the knot

ULTIMATE

WEDDING

PLANNER

CARLEY RONEY

& the editors of The Knot.com

the knot

ULTIMATE

WEDDING

PLANNER

Worksheets, Checklists, Etiquette, Calendars, &

Answers to Frequently Asked Questions

www.theknot.com
AOL keyword: knot

Broadway Books New York

BROADWAY

PRINTED IN THE UNITED STATES OF AMERICA.

BROADWAY BOOKS and its logo, a letter B bisected on the diagonal, are trademarks of Broadway Books, a division of Random House, Inc.

The Knot, TheKnot.com, and its logo are trademarks of The Knot, Inc.

First edition published 1999

Visit our website at www.broadwaybooks.com

Designed by Judith Stagnitto Abbate / Abbate Design

Cataloging-in-Publication Data is on file with the Library of Congress.

ISBN 0-7679-0247-5

10 9 8

contents

acknowledgments

This book would be nothing without the terrifyingly talented team at **The Knot.com**. Everyone who has helped research, write, produce, code, or otherwise build the #1 wedding website should be credited here. A special thanks to Tracy Guth for pulling together the original edition of this book and to Julie Raimondi for producing this update.

Many wise and talented industry experts and photographers contributed to this book. They are great resources for couples planning weddings, and so we have included their complete contact information in the Appendix. I can't thank them enough for their insights and images.

The millions of brides and grooms and their families that use TheKnot.com are my most important partners. They have taught me more about weddings than I could learn in a lifetime. I thank them for their constant input and ideas.

Most of all, I'd be nowhere without the love of my darling husband (and The Knot CEO), David Liu, the inspiration of my dear sweet daughter, Havana Rose, and the support of my families near and far.

Thank you one and all.

operating instructions

HOW TO USE THIS BOOK

Producing a wedding involves endless details, pressing deadlines, family drama, and—far too often—enough stress to kill any prenuptial honeymoon period. *The Knot Ultimate Wedding Planner* is a couple's secret weapon against such insanity. It's your cheat sheet—telling you what you need to know and do, and when. It's your insider's guide—giving you TheKnot.com's most essential expert advice in bite-size pieces. It's your security blanket—the next best thing to a guarantee that you'll have a memorable wedding without losing your mind.

Here's how to get the most out of these jam-packed pages:

Don't Leave Home Without It
You never know when someone will mention an amazing caterer or you'll remember a must-not-forget name for your guest list. Take this book with you everywhere. Jot down all your wedding notes in one place (use the inside covers if you run out of room in the notes areas). Must-have accessories include a pen, a small spiral-bound notebook, and a heavyweight two-pocket folder—label one side Research, the other Completed Contracts. (Since we're all on the go, we aren't fans of the fifteen-pound planner, but if you think you'll be tearing out tons of magazine pages and collecting piles of brochures, you may want a three-ring binder or accordion file.)

Use Your Imagination
Before you get overwhelmed by all the minutiae, sit down together and read Chapter 2, "Getting Started." It's meant to get your juices flowing with a worksheet to help you envision exactly what kind of wedding you want to have. Keep an open mind and have some fun with it; your answers will inform future detail

decisions. You'll also need to finalize a budget before you spend a dime—our easy worksheet on page 14 will lead you through it.

Stay on Schedule

Chapter 1 is an overall wedding-planning calendar and checklist that lays out the entire process and tells you what to do when. Read it all the way through before you begin to get a sense of the timing involved. To personalize it, backtrack from your wedding date and fill in the actual deadlines: one month before, two months before, and so on. The calendar also refers you to the chapters in this book that get into detail on specific topics.

Do Your Homework

The worksheets at the start of each chapter will help you focus your thoughts and create a vision for each aspect of your wedding. Have everyone involved in the decision making help with these exercises to make sure you're all on the same page before you begin. Once you have an idea of what you're looking for, you'll need to find professionals to handle the task. Don't hire anyone until you've asked each and every question on the lists in each chapter. The answers will clue you in to how professionals approach their work—and to whether their approach is appropriate for your wedding.

Take Our Advice

In each chapter we share our most essential Knot Knowledge—what we've learned in our years of experience talking to wedding professionals and hundreds of thousands of brides and grooms. Read these essential tips and money-saving tricks; then peruse the "Ask Carley" sections for up-to-date answers to the most frequently asked questions in each category before you make any final decisions. For our comprehensive advice—and unlimited ideas—be sure to get a copy of our companion reference, the 450-page *The Knot Complete Guide to Weddings in the Real World,* and, of course, you'll want to log on to our highly acclaimed Web site at **www.TheKnot.com** and AOL keyword: **Knot**.

Delve into Detail

The latter part of each chapter gets into the specifics of executing your plan. Use our checklists to make sure your contracts with each vendor are complete. Fill in the contact cheat sheet for each professional you hire—you'll need easy access to their information as other vendors request it or when it's needed in an emergency. (Hint: Staple business cards to each vendor's contact page. It will help you turn to them easily.)

Have It Your Way

This book is about realistic guidelines, not hard-and-fast rules. Feel free to personalize the process according to your own priorities. If photography means everything to you, by all means secure your photographer and spend 10 percent of your budget on your package instead of the suggested 8 percent (just make sure it all still adds up to 100 percent). Same goes for etiquette: We give you the guidelines, but you need to judge your own situation.

Enjoy the Ride

Okay, we admit it: Planning a wedding can be a roller-coaster ride. But considering this is likely to be the most extravagant party you'll ever throw in your lives, you'd better have a blast—from your first hour brainstorming right through the last five seconds of your reception. We'll help, of course, but you're ultimately responsible for delighting in every up and riding out every down. Some general advice: Don't drive yourself insane over every detail. Declare some days wedding-free zones. And, most of all, maintain your sense of humor. Laughter will go a long way toward keeping the love bug alive throughout the planning process.

the knot

ULTIMATE

WEDDING

PLANNER

---

a month–by–month checklist

This checklist will guide you through the major to-dos of planning a wedding. We've based it on a yearlong engagement. If you have more time, lucky you. Hire your most important professionals, especially if they are in high demand, as early as you can. If you have less time, just start at the beginning and get busy; you'll need to be more decisive. Cross out any to-dos that don't relate to you, and add your extras at the end. See the relevant chapters (noted in parentheses) for more detailed breakdowns of your to-dos on that topic. We're off!

12+ Months Before (or ASAP)

- ☐ Meet, call, or e-mail important friends and family with the big news. Parents of the bride traditionally come first.

- ☐ Envision your overall wedding. (Use the worksheet on pages 10–11.)

- ☐ Draw up your wedding budget with help from your families. (Use the worksheet on page 14.)

- ☐ Choose several options for date and time. (See page 10.)

- ☐ Ask close friends and relatives to be members of the wedding party. (See Chapter 3.)

- ☐ Hire your wedding consultant.

- ☐ Decide on your wedding size and start drawing up the initial guest list. (See pages 188–92.)

- ☐ Start researching ceremony and reception sites. (See Chapters 4 and 5.)

- ☐ Book any vendors you have already decided upon or are completely focused on—after you make sure they suit your budget.

- ☐ Book your ceremony and reception locations. (See pages 41 and 53.)

- ☐ If the priest, minister, or rabbi at a house of worship isn't marrying you, choose and book an officiant. (See page 37.)

- ☐ Make a Web page to announce your wedding. (Go to **www.TheKnot.com**.) You may also choose to announce your engagement in the newspapers.

- ☐ Have an engagement party (optional). (You may want to register for gifts beforehand; see Chapter 8.)

8–10 Months Before (By date: _____/_____/_____)

- ☐ Bride: Start envisioning and shopping for your dress. (See Chapter 6.)

- ☐ Envision your wedding food; start researching and interviewing caterers. (See Chapter 7.)

- ☐ Start researching and interviewing photographers and videographers. (See Chapters 11 and 12.)

- ☐ Envision your wedding entertainment; start researching and interviewing reception bands or DJs. (See Chapter 9.)

- ☐ Picture your floral decor; start researching and interviewing florists. (See Chapter 14.)

- ☐ If you're marrying during a tourist or holiday season or having a destination wedding, send a save-the-date card to guests.

- ☐ If you'll have many out-of-town guests, research and reserve accommodations. (See page 28.)
- ☐ Book your caterer. (See pages 76–77.)
- ☐ Bride: Order your wedding dress. (See page 62.)
- ☐ Register for gifts. (See Chapter 8.)
- ☐ If you'll need to rent anything for your ceremony or reception (chairs, tables, tent, and so on), contact a rental company.
- ☐ Book your photographer. (See page 118.)
- ☐ Book your videographer. (See page 126.)
- ☐ Book your reception band or DJ. (See page 97.)
- ☐ Book your florist. (See pages 142–43.)

6–8 Months Before (By date: _____/_____/_____)

- ☐ Decide on your menu.
- ☐ Book your ceremony musicians. (See page 96.)
- ☐ Start shopping for bridesmaids' dresses. (See Chapter 10.)
- ☐ Finalize flower ideas with florist.
- ☐ Start planning your honeymoon. (See Chapter 13.)
- ☐ Order the bridesmaids' dresses. (See page 106.)
- ☐ Start working on your songlists for the ceremony (page 90) and reception (pages 90–91).

4–6 Months Before (By date: _____/_____/_____)

- ☐ Attend prewedding counseling (if required).
- ☐ Start shopping for invitations. (See Chapter 15.)
- ☐ Groom: Start shopping for your and the groomsmen's formalwear. (See Chapter 17.)
- ☐ If necessary, get passports for your honeymoon.
- ☐ Start shopping for wedding rings. (See page 42.)
- ☐ Envision your wedding cake; start researching and interviewing cake designers. (See Chapter 16.)

3 Months Before (By date: _____/_____/_____)

☐ Finalize your guest list.

☐ Order your invitations. (See pages 150–151.)

☐ Order your wedding cake. (See page 158.)

☐ Order your wedding rings.

☐ Hire a calligrapher if you want your invitations professionally addressed.

☐ Attend your shower (may be earlier, depending on when your hosts decide to have it).

☐ Groom: Rent the men's formalwear. (See page 165.)

☐ Hire limousines/other cars for transport on wedding day. (See Chapter 18.)

2 Months Before (By date: _____/_____/_____)

☐ Mail your invitations.

☐ If you'll say original vows, write them.

☐ Purchase gifts for parents, attendants, and each other.

☐ Find and meet with a makeup artist for a trial run or get a makeover at a department-store counter and purchase any products you need.

☐ Make an appointment with your hairstylist to try out big-day dos.

1 Month Before (By date: _____/_____/_____)

☐ Bride: Have your final wedding dress fitting. Bring your maid of honor along so she can learn how to bustle your dress. Have the dress pressed and bring it home.

☐ Call all bridesmaids to make sure they have their gowns ready for the wedding (or that they're in the process of having alterations done).

☐ Before your florist places your order, be sure that you're happy with all the flowers and arrangements you've chosen; make last-minute adjustments.

☐ If you want a groom's cake and/or other pastries or desserts, talk to your cake designer to discuss your additions.

☐ If you want a wedding program (and you didn't order a printed one with your invitations), write it, format it on your computer, and make copies for all your guests.

☐ Order or plan in-room welcome baskets—fruit, chocolate, bottled water, and other treats, plus a welcome note and an additional copy of directions to the sites—for out-of-town guests' hotel rooms.

Two Weeks & Counting

☐ Apply for a marriage license together in the town where you'll wed. (See page 43; you may need to go three weeks before.)

☐ Call guests who have not yet returned their invitation response cards.

☐ Deliver a must-take photo list to the photographer, including who should be in formal portraits. Determine when portraits will be shot (before or after the ceremony, or during the reception).

☐ Draw up and deliver to your DJ or bandleader a list of special song requests, and any songs you definitely want or *don't* want played.

☐ If needed, give your videographer a must-shoot list.

☐ Bride: Get one last prewedding haircut or trim and hair color touch-up.

1 Week Before

☐ Give the reception site and the caterer a final guest head count; include vendors, such as band members and the photographer, who will expect a meal. (Also, ask how many extra plates the caterer will prepare; that is, the plate count.)

☐ Supply the reception site manager with a list of requests from other vendors (such as a table for the DJ, setup space needed by the florist, and so on).

☐ Do the reception seating chart and write out place or table cards.

☐ Call professionals to confirm all arrangements and confirm a wedding-day (home or mobile) phone number for each:

Officiant ceremony site contact	Phone: _____
Ceremony musicians	Phone: _____
Reception site	Phone: _____
Caterer	Phone: _____
Florist	Phone: _____
Photographer	Phone: _____
Videographer	Phone: _____
Cake designer/baker	Phone: _____
Limousine or rental-car company	Phone: _____

☐ Give the ceremony and reception site managers a schedule of vendor delivery and setup times, plus contact numbers.

- [ ] Groom: Get your hair trimmed.
- [ ] Attend bachelor/bachelorette parties.

2–3 Days Before

- [ ] Bride: If your dress still needs to be pressed or steamed, do this now.
- [ ] Groom: Go in for a final fitting and pick up your formalwear.
- [ ] Ask the best man to make sure all groomsmen go for fittings and pick up their outfits.
- [ ] Touch base with the ceremony and reception sites one more time.
- [ ] In preparation for the rehearsal, determine the order of bridesmaids and groomsmen in the processional and recessional.
- [ ] If the caterer will be arranging place cards, table cards, menu cards, or disposable cameras, hand them off.
- [ ] Reconfirm that the florist received your (correct) flower order (discuss any necessary last-minute substitutions) and knows where and when the flowers should be delivered. Should the personal flowers go to the ceremony site or to your home?
- [ ] Call the limousine or rental-car company to reconfirm locations and pickup times.
- [ ] Arrange for guests who will not rent cars to be picked up from the airport or train station. Ask local friends, attendants, or relatives to help.
- [ ] Put welcome baskets in out-of-town guests' hotel rooms (get attendants to help).
- [ ] Get a manicure and/or pedicure.

Day Before

- [ ] Make sure all wedding professionals have an emergency phone number to call on the day of the wedding.
- [ ] Write checks and/or talk to the wedding hosts (usually your parents, if not you) about final balances to be paid at the end of the reception.
- [ ] Meet your wedding party, ceremony readers, immediate family, and officiant at the ceremony site to rehearse the ceremony.
- [ ] Bring the unity candle, aisle runner, yarmulkes, or other ceremony accessories to the site, so you won't have to think about them on the wedding morning.
- [ ] Give your marriage license to your officiant.

☐ Attend your rehearsal dinner.

☐ Present attendants with their gifts at the rehearsal dinner (especially if they are accessories to be worn during the wedding).

☐ Get a good night's sleep!

Day Of

☐ Present parents (and each other) with gifts or at least a big hug and kiss.

☐ Give the best man and/or maid of honor your wedding bands.

☐ Give the best man the officiant's fee envelope, to be handed off after the ceremony.

☐ Hook up your reception site manager and your wedding consultant or maid of honor so they can deal with any questions or problems during the party.

☐ Assign a family member or attendant to be the photographer's contact.

☐ Remember to thoroughly enjoy yourselves at the reception.

☐ Arrange for someone to return rental supplies that didn't get sent back directly from the site the Monday after the wedding.

☐ Arrange for honor attendants to take your dress to the dry cleaner and tux to the rental shop the Monday after the wedding.

Postwedding

☐ If you were pleased by the work of your wedding vendors, send each a thank-you note (and a picture or two of their work, if possible).

☐ When you return from your honeymoon, make sure to call and thank each of your attendants one more time.

☐ Keep a gift log (see pages 193–97) and send out those thank-you notes as soon as possible.

☐ Log on to **www.TheKnot.com** and report what you loved most about your wedding and what, if anything, you'd do differently.

☐ Celebrate your one-month anniversary in style.

Notes

_____

_____

_____

_____

_____

_____

_____

_____

_____

_____

_____

_____

_____

_____

_____

_____

_____

_____

_____

_____

_____

_____

_____

_____

_____

_____

_____

_____

getting started

Once you announce your wedding, everyone in the world will have opinions for you. Before that happens, make sure you spend some time together—just the two of you—trying to discover your own wedding vision. Be clear—right from the start—as to who will be involved in making decisions and how the tasks of planning will be divided. Brace yourself for a little inevitable family drama. But most of all, enjoy yourselves in these early weeks: If you aren't having a formal engagement party, use the excuse to go out and celebrate often with friends.

Your Wedding Vision Worksheet

Chances are you have some vision of what your wedding will be like. Sit down and fill out this worksheet together (or make a copy for each of you so your answers aren't skewed).

Describe the event (check all that apply)

- ☐ Intimate
- ☐ Formal
- ☐ Relaxed
- ☐ Elegant
- ☐ Untraditional
- ☐ Religious
- ☐ Over the top

- ☐ Grand
- ☐ Casual
- ☐ Festive
- ☐ Traditional
- ☐ Ethnic
- ☐ Theme

Locale
- ☐ Where you live
- ☐ Bride's hometown

- ☐ Away from home
- ☐ Groom's hometown

Size
- ☐ Intimate (<100)
- ☐ Large (250+)

- ☐ Average (100–250)

Approx. # of guests_____

Season
- ☐ Spring/Summer

- ☐ Fall/Winter

Hour
- ☐ Sunrise
- ☐ Midday
- ☐ Sunset

- ☐ Evening
- ☐ Late night

Choices of date: 1st _____/_____/_____ 2nd _____/_____/_____

Choices of time: 1st _____ 2nd _____

Palette
- ☐ Spring pastels
- ☐ Black and white
- ☐ Citrus hues

- ☐ All white
- ☐ Rich winter hues
- ☐ Metallic

Specific colors: _____

_____

Festivities (check all that apply)

- ☐ Engagement party
- ☐ Bachelorette party
- ☐ Couple shower
- ☐ Wedding-eve party

- ☐ Shower or luncheon
- ☐ Bachelor party
- ☐ Rehearsal dinner
- ☐ Postreception party

Your priorities (rank from 1 to 10)

_____ Time of year/day of week
_____ Officiant or ceremony location
_____ Guest list (emphasis: family or friends?)
_____ Food & drink
_____ Music
_____ Reception location (proximity or type)
_____ Attire (the bride's dress)
_____ Ambiance (flowers and decor)
_____ Mementos (photo and videos)
_____ Other _____

Opinions that count (check all that apply; asterisk * who has final word)

☐ Bride and groom   ☐ Friends and attendants
☐ Bride's parents   ☐ Groom's parents
☐ Other _____

Planning committee (check all that apply; asterisk * who is in charge)

☐ Bride   ☐ Groom
☐ Bride's parents   ☐ Friends and attendants
☐ Groom's parents   ☐ Wedding coordinator
☐ Other _____

Special interests or highlights in your relationship story that can help inspire your wedding details (you both love books; you met in New Orleans during Mardi Gras; you drank martinis on your first date; he proposed holding a big box of doughnuts, or M&Ms, or daisies . . .)

_____

_____

_____

_____

_____

_____

_____

_____

_____

_____

_____

Ways to Save No matter how big, a budget is still a budget, and you will always need to save somewhere. There are five basic strategies for slicing your spending while still planning an inspiring wedding:

1. *Cut down.* Invite 100 guests instead of 150; serve three courses instead of five; have two bridesmaids instead of ten.
2. *Loosen up.* The less formal the affair, the more affordable. Instead of a sit-down hotel dinner, go for a casual brunch or barbecue.
3. *Pick and choose.* Indulge in a designer dress but go barefoot; serve a great cake and skip the dessert table.
4. *Put it off.* Get silver wedding bands and upgrade to platinum on your first anniversary; exchange gifts at the six-month mark.
5. *Do it yourself.* Never underestimate the penny-pinching power of elbow grease. Coordinate the alcohol, make favors, address your own envelopes.

Make a Statement Cookie-cutter weddings are definitively out. Be creative. Use your relationship history, heritage, favorite colors, or activities as inspiration for a more personal party.

Pick Your Battles Don't obsess over every single detail. Win the wedding war by spending your budget, energy, and attention on the things that matter most to you. (Decide on your priorities with the worksheet at the start of this chapter.)

Smarten Up Weddings are a whole new world with its very own lingo. Read up on each category so you and your vendor are speaking vaguely the same language. TheKnot.com and *The Knot's Complete Guide to Weddings in the Real World* are good places to begin.

Play Dumb Don't ever be afraid that your questions are too stupid. Don't act as though you know things you don't. Don't hire anyone until you've got a good answer to every question listed in the relevant chapter of this book.

Trust Yourself Textbook etiquette does not apply to all. Become familiar with the rules, but you decide whether they apply to your reality.

Get It in Writing You're spending a lot of money. Protect yourself by making sure all details are down on paper and signed by both parties. Contract points for each vendor are delineated in each chapter; check off each list before you sign.

Pay Properly Every time you make any kind of payment, do the following: (1) If no invoice is provided, draw up a letter noting the date, the payment amount, exactly what the payment is supposed to cover, the check number, and so on. Keep a copy for yourself. (2) Make a copy of every check you write and get credit-card receipts. Staple these to your invoice or letter and keep them in your folder.

Use a Credit Card If the terms of the contract you draw up with a professional are not met, you can call your credit-card company and dispute payment. If you pay in

KERRY & JOHN: LONG-DISTANCE PLANNING

July 27
Baltimore, Maryland
Planning Time Frame: One Year and a Half

FOR KERRY AND JOHN, planning a wedding 750 miles from where they intended to get married was quite an undertaking. "I discovered the two most important and successful elements to long-distance planning were to start as early as possible and be very organized," says Kerry.

With a wedding date set for a full year and a half after the engagement, Kerry and John were able to plan their Baltimore, Maryland, garden-style celebration from Chicago, Illinois, with relative ease. By the time the couple moved from Baltimore to Chicago, one year before the wedding, they had booked their ceremony location, reception site, officiant, photographer, and videographer. With those megadetails firmly in place, Kerry was able to focus on the other elements (her gown, the flowers, the music, the menu, and the invitations) one baby step at a time.

For the next year, Kerry and John corresponded with vendors through e-mails, long-distance phone calls, and quick trips to Maryland every other month. With a notebook (and a series of pressing questions) in hand, Kerry and John carefully narrowed their search until only one vendor was left in each category. Though Kerry and John planned the wedding without the help of a consultant, they credit each vendor with playing a significant role in making their dream wedding a reality. "Looking back, the year and a half of planning was quite exhausting," says Kerry. "But, our wedding day couldn't have been more perfect and even surpassed both my husband's and my expectations."

Kerry & John's Long-Distance Planning Tips

- BE RESOURCEFUL. Utilize as many resources as you can: the Internet, local planning guides, wedding magazines, friends or family recently married in the same area, or even the local library. Research, research, research—the more ideas you bring to the table the easier it will be for your vendors to plan a wedding day that suits your needs, desires, and, most important, your personalities.
- BE EFFICIENT. If you have to fly back and forth from your home to the wedding site, try to combine work and pleasure on your stays so wedding planning does not become a burden. Also, learn to communicate via e-mail or sign up for a cost-effective long-distance phone plan so contacting vendors doesn't cost you an unnecessary fortune.
- BE RESPECTFUL. Developing a relationship with your vendors is key. Be punctual, thoughtful, and considerate of their time. Trust their expertise and ask them for recommendations of other vendors you may be able to use. (And don't forget to send them thank-you notes for all of their hard work!)

cash, you don't have any recourse. There's no need to inherently distrust your wedding professionals, of course, but you'll want to protect your investment, as you would with any other big-ticket item. Be aware that some professionals won't take credit cards; ask when you agree to work together. Make sure the credit card you do use accumulates frequent-flyer miles—your wedding charges may just cover your honeymoon flight.

Check References Never sign a contract with a vendor before you call past clients and, as a backup, the Better Business Bureau (www.bbb.org). Demand recent references—from the past year. Ask references detailed questions, such as: Were there any charges on your final bill that you did not expect? Would you have preferred that the vendor have done anything differently? Were the courses served (or flowers used, or songs played) what you had decided on?

Goof Off A crash diet consisting only of wedding planning can kill the mood. Declare wedding-free zones—nights out with each other where all talk of table cards and canapes is completely forbidden.

Can You Coordinate? Hire a wedding consultant if: (1) neither you nor your families (read: moms) have time to plan your wedding; (2) neither you nor your families have any *desire* to plan your wedding; (3) you're planning a wedding out of town; or (4) you simply prefer—and can afford—professional help. They'll do the legwork, hire vendors, negotiate your contracts, and may even save you some money. Expect to pay 10 to 15 percent of your total wedding budget. Call the Association of Bridal Consultants (860-355-0464) for a referral.

Wedding Budget Worksheet

Don't drive yourselves or your family into debt over your wedding! Use this formula to help you figure out how much money you can save or your families can contribute. These estimates are not for everyone. You need to assess your other financial pressures, such as loans, debt, and so on, before you fix on a number.

Your existing savings:
    (Value of liquid savings) $_____ x .50 = $_____

Your saving potential:
    (Combined monthly income $_____ x .20)
    x (# of months of engagement) = $_____

Bride's parents' contribution (if applicable): $_____

Groom's parents' contribution (if applicable): $_____

                Total budget: $_____

Budget Estimates by Category

Before you can begin talking to any vendors, you need to know approximately how much of your budget you can spend in each category. Here are some averages to help you get some figures in mind. In this example, the reception is the biggest priority; your priorities may be different, so feel free to move percentages and money around accordingly. Use the budget worksheet in the Appendix to track your actual expenses through the process.

Total budget $_____

Category	%	Example Wedding ($30,000)	Your Estimates
Reception site, rentals, food, drink, cake	x .48	$14,400	$_____
Bride & groom's attire	x .10	$3,000	$_____
Flowers & decorations	x .08	$2,400	$_____
Photo & video	x .12	$3,600	$_____
Music & entertainment	x .08	$2,400	$_____
Invitations & stationery	x .03	$900	$_____
Ceremony site & officiant	x .03	$900	$_____
Wedding rings	x .03	$900	$_____
Attendant gifts	x .03	$900	$_____
Transportation & parking	x .02	$600	$_____

Factor in 5–10 percent for unforseen items, overages, taxes, and tips.

Note that the following big-ticket items are not included: honeymoon (can run upward of $3,000); wedding consultant (up to 10 percent of total budget); rehearsal dinner.

SHERI & SCOTT: WORKING WITH A WEDDING CONSULTANT

August 16
Chicago
Planning Time Frame: One Year

WHEN SHERI AND SCOTT GOT ENGAGED, she was working at a public relations firm in Atlanta while he attended dental school in Augusta, Georgia, two hours away. Only seeing each other on weekends, the couple knew something about long-distance planning. When they decided to get married in Chicago, where the bride grew up, Sheri chose to hire a wedding consultant. Her parents were moving back to Illinois a few months before the wedding, so for the majority of the planning time no family lived in the wedding city. "Because I work in PR, I know how challenging planning a special event can be, especially one that's out of state," Sheri says. "I wanted an expert who could take charge when I couldn't."

Sheri hired a consultant for $1,200. The planning required trips to Chicago. About a year before the wedding, Scott and Shari went to meet the consultant and see reception sites. "She was great." Sheri explains, "We had appointments at every upscale hotel in the city in one day!" The couple also listened to wedding bands and looked at churches. A few months later, Sheri and her mother returned to meet with photographers and to book the reception site, the Mid-America Club, on the scenic eightieth floor of the Standard Oil Building. Sheri's final planning trip was in May, three months before the big day, to meet with florists, have a tasting at the reception site, and attend her first shower.

Shari and Scott's Consultant Tips

- You retain veto power. Just because a consultant refers you to certain wedding vendors doesn't mean you must hire them. You'll just have to do a bit of additional research. "That's how I found a videographer," Sheri says. "I had sample videos sent to me in Atlanta and I narrowed it down. Then the consultant went to meet with them and helped me choose one."
- Expect the consultant to be in your corner. Before you sign the contract, make sure she will help if you experience problems with a vendor that she has recommended.
- Use the consultant as an extra ear. "Not only did my consultant help plan the wedding, she also acted as a friend who offered advice," says Sheri.

Wedding-Planning Etiquette

Q: How long should our engagement be?

A: There is no "right" engagement length. Some people get married in three months, some in three years. The longer you have before your wedding date, the better chance you'll get the best vendors. Start nailing down your date, sites, and most important vendors ASAP. Another great reason for a long engagement is to save up wedding funds. (See worksheet on page 14.) If your wedding is years off, keep in mind that some places may not take reservations until two years in advance. If it's mere months until your desired date, don't hesitate to call around and see what and who are available; last-minute cancellations do happen.

Q: Who is expected to pay for what these days?

A: Nowadays the couple and both sets of parents contribute to the wedding coffer. (The couple footing the entire bill themselves is also common.) Assess your own savings (see the worksheet on page 14). Powwow with both sets of parents (separately) to find out how much they can contribute. It is then up to you, the couple, to take charge and decide how to divvy up all the expenses and responsibilities. Never assume contributions are coming unless you've talked about it. Never demand that people cover particular expenses.

Keep in mind that every family has different views on all this, and it particularly differs from culture to culture. In American weddings, this is how it has traditionally been broken down: The bride and her family pay for the ceremony site and accessories; reception site and all professional party services; floral arrangements for ceremony and reception, plus bouquets for bridesmaids and flower girls; invitations, announcements, and other stationery; bride's dress, veil, and accessories; photography and videography; and transportation of wedding party to ceremony and reception sites. The groom and his family cover the wedding rings; rehearsal dinner; groom's wedding clothes; bride's bouquet, boutonnieres, and corsages; marriage license and officiant's fee; and honeymoon.

Q: If our parents pay, do they get to decide everything?

A: Be clear from the very beginning about who has a say in your wedding decisions and who will have the final word. If your parents are paying, you can expect they will have extra interest, just as you would if it were your money. The best way to keep control issues clear is to designate particular areas of power to each person: "Mom, you are paying for [read: dictating] the flowers." "Dad, your contribution will go toward the wine." Give up control in areas you care less about, and keep control over (which will most likely involve paying for) those areas that mean the world to you. If your parents are the type to give you free rein, be thankful.

Q: We are on a very tight budget. Is it okay to ask for contributions from our guests?

A: Never consider charging your wedding guests admission (asking for money of any kind). If you need contributions, take them in kind: Have a casual picnic wedding and make it a potluck, asking each person to bring his or her favorite dish. Ask to borrow a family friend's fancy car in lieu of a wedding gift. People love to help out, but they'll be offended if your invitation has a price tag.

Q: Who throws the engagement party? Is it okay to invite people who won't be invited to the wedding?

A: It's the bride's family's prerogative to throw the first engagement party; after they have done so (or determined not to), the groom's family gets a turn. Some couples plan their own laid-back bash with friends and close relatives at a favorite bar or restaurant. Gifts are optional, but because many guests do choose to give them, you'll want to register beforehand. Do your best not to invite people who won't be wedding guests.

staple business card here

CONTACT CHEAT SHEET:
Wedding Consultant

Name: _____

Address: _____

_____

Phone: _____

Fax: _____

E-mail: _____

Total cost $ _____

Deposit $ _____   Date paid: ____/____/____

Balance $ _____   Date due: ____/____/____

Notes

_____

_____

_____

_____

_____

_____

_____

_____

_____

_____

_____

_____

_____

_____

_____

_____

_____

_____

_____

attendants, family, & guests

M odern weddings can have five guests or five hundred, only honor attendants or teams of seven on each side. Guys can be bridesmaids, and a dog can do the duties of the ring bearer. To avoid hurt feelings, make it clear *early* what style of involvement by family and friends your heart is set on. Also, never assume everyone knows what they are supposed to do when you assign them their title. Be clear about your expectations of friends, parents, and other family.

Attendants & Guests Worksheet

Total guest list # _____

Who gets to invite how many guests:

Bride and groom   #_____   Bride's parents   #_____

Groom's parents   #_____   Already included #_____
                                 (for example, officiant & wife)

Ceremony roles

Which of the following (and how many of each) would you like to have? Jot down names where obvious.

☐ Bride's honor attendant _____

☐ Bride's attendants (#_____)   _____

_____   _____

_____   _____

_____   _____

☐ Groom's honor attendant _____

☐ Groom's attendants (#_____)   _____

_____   _____

_____   _____

_____   _____

☐ Additional ushers (#_____)   _____

_____   _____

☐ Ring bearer _____

☐ Flower girl(s) _____

☐ Reader(s)/Performer(s) _____

_____

☐ Other (assistants needed for holding huppah, handing out programs or flower petals, lighting candles, helping perform other religious or ethnic rituals, and so on)

_____

_____

Attendant Etiquette

Q: Do I have to have my groom's sister in my wedding party?

A: It's not mandatory to have his sister as a bridesmaid or her brother as a groomsman, but keep in mind that in some families this is expected. It might be easier to keep the peace by agreeing to it. (Two months of discomfort is better than two years of the cold shoulder.) Or, as is the trend these days, consider having your opposite-sex siblings stand up on your own side (see below).

Q: Can a best friend of the opposite sex stand up on the "wrong" side?

A: Definitely! If a bride wants a male pal as her attendant, she can call him the man of honor or bridesman (a groom's female friend would be the best maid or a groomswoman). More and more couples are asking close friends of the opposite sex to stand up for them, and you know, it's about time. It's no secret these days that women and men can be friends!

Q: Is there a difference between a groomsman and an usher, or are they the same thing?

A: The terms *usher* and *groomsman* can mean the same thing, but they don't have to. It used to be the norm (and still is in some communities and families) that the groomsmen—those guys who stand next to the groom—also served as ushers, seating guests as they arrived at the ceremony. So the terms became interchangeable. However, these days friends or relatives other than the groomsmen are often asked to usher.

Q: Is it appropriate for relatives to host a shower? Isn't it considered improper because it's as though the relatives are asking for gifts for the bride?

A: Having a mom, sister, and/or other relative throw a bridal shower is no longer the biggest wedding faux pas ever, probably for the simple reason that it's practical. More brides and grooms are living in places other than where they grew up, and their attendants may be from all over the country. It's just not realistic to expect a maid of honor in Seattle to plan a shower in Chicago without any help from the locals. Often Mom or Sis is the one in the wedding city who can really coordinate shower plans. Faraway bridesmaids and honor attendants are definitely pitching in, but more and more, Mom's party is central. In fact, showers thrown by relatives are pretty much the norm in some regions of the country.

Q: What do attendants pay for?

A: Attendants are generally responsible for all their wedding-day expenses: their clothes and accessories, hair and makeup, transportation to the wedding city, and lodging once they're there. Usually they also purchase shower and wedding presents. Not easy on the wallet, is it? If you're concerned about your attendants' budgets, research discount airfares or arrange for local attendants to have out-of-towners stay with them; offer to pay for your attendants' dresses or tuxes as their thank-you gift. Another generous option. Tell them that their participation is the only wedding present you want.

BRIDE'S HONOR ATTENDANT CHEAT SHEET

Prewedding

- ☐ Help bride shop for gown
- ☐ Help bride shop for bridesmaids' dresses
- ☐ Spread word about couple's registry
- ☐ Coordinate bridesmaids' dress order, payment, fittings, and dressing
- ☐ Plan shower and/or bachelorette party
- ☐ Offer assistance with planning tasks
- ☐ Arrange bridesmaids' travel and lodging
- ☐ Create a wedding-day emergency kit
- ☐ Attend rehearsal dinner
- ☐ Organize bridesmaids on wedding day

At ceremony

- ☐ Walk down the aisle directly before the bride (if no flower girl)
- ☐ Adjust bride's train at altar
- ☐ Hold her bouquet during the vows
- ☐ Carry groom's wedding ring
- ☐ Walk in recessional with best man
- ☐ Organize programs, tossing petals, and so on
- ☐ Sign marriage license as a witness

At reception

- ☐ May stand in receiving line
- ☐ Help bride bustle her gown
- ☐ May sit at head table next to groom
- ☐ May MC or make toast to the couple
- ☐ Help "host" party (make introductions, get people dancing, and so on)
- ☐ Dance with best man during first dance (if wedding party is involved)
- ☐ Help direct vendors—caterer, photographer, band—as needed

Postwedding

- ☐ Help organize postreception party
- ☐ Help take care of gifts and gift checks brought to the reception
- ☐ Take bride's gown to the dry cleaner

Other _____

_____

_____

GROOM'S HONOR ATTENDANT CHEAT SHEET

Prewedding

- ☐ Help groom shop for formalwear
- ☐ Coordinate tux fittings and payments
- ☐ Plan the couple's shower and/or bachelor party
- ☐ Spread word about couple's registry
- ☐ Offer assistance with planning tasks
- ☐ Arrange groomsmen's travel and lodging
- ☐ Attend rehearsal dinner
- ☐ Organize groomsmen on wedding day

At ceremony

- ☐ Stand at front with groom and other groomsmen as procession begins (or walk in, in a Jewish ceremony)
- ☐ Carry bride's (or both) wedding ring(s)
- ☐ Walk in recessional with bride's honor attendant
- ☐ Sign marriage license as a witness
- ☐ Give officiant his or her fee

At reception

- ☐ May stand in receiving line
- ☐ May sit at head table next to bride
- ☐ Serve as toastmaster, making first toast to couple
- ☐ Dance with maid of honor during first dance (if wedding party is involved)
- ☐ Help "host" party (make introductions, get people dancing, and so on)
- ☐ Help direct vendors—caterer, photographer, band—as needed
- ☐ Help groom give out final payments and tips to vendors
- ☐ Collect gifts and gift checks brought to the reception

Postwedding

- ☐ Help organize postreception party
- ☐ Drive newlyweds to their wedding-night hotel or the airport
- ☐ Return all tuxes to rental shop

Other _____

_____

_____

Photocopy, cut out, and give to appropriate parties

BRIDESMAID CHEAT SHEET

Prewedding
- ☐ May help bride shop for her dress
- ☐ Unless an out-of-town maid, goes on at least one bridesmaid-dress-shopping trip
- ☐ Go for fittings and alterations as needed
- ☐ Help with wedding-planning errands
- ☐ Help plan shower and/or bachelorette party

At ceremony
- ☐ Along with other bridesmaids, walk single file in the procession
- ☐ Stand in line in front of altar or stage, or sit in front pew with other bridesmaids
- ☐ Walk in recessional paired with a groomsman

At reception
- ☐ May be announced at reception
- ☐ May sit at head table
- ☐ Take part in first dance (if entire wedding party is involved)

Other
_____
_____
_____
_____

GROOMSMAN CHEAT SHEET

Prewedding
- ☐ May help groom choose formalwear
- ☐ Go for fittings and alterations as needed
- ☐ Attend couple's shower, if there will be one
- ☐ Help plan, and attend, bachelor party

At ceremony
- ☐ If you will also serve as an usher, stand at door ready to escort guests to their seats
- ☐ Stand with groom, best man, and other groomsmen at the altar or stage as ceremony is about to begin
- ☐ Stand in line or sit in front pew with other groomsmen during ceremony
- ☐ Walk in recessional paired with a bridesmaid

At reception
- ☐ May be announced at reception
- ☐ May sit at head table
- ☐ Take part in first dance (if entire wedding party is involved)

Other
_____
_____
_____
_____

FLOWER GIRL CHEAT SHEET

- ☐ Attend shower with mother
- ☐ Walk in processional directly before the bride (possibly with ring bearer), carrying a bouquet, wearing a floral head wreath, and/or scattering flower petals from a basket
- ☐ Sit with parents during the ceremony and at the reception

Other
_____
_____
_____
_____

RING BEARER CHEAT SHEET

- ☐ Walk in processional directly before the bride (possibly with flower girl), carrying a ring pillow with the "wedding bands" (most couples entrust the real ones to the honor attendants)
- ☐ Sit with parents during the ceremony and at the reception

Other
_____
_____
_____
_____
_____

Photocopy, cut out, and give to appropriate parties

MOTHER OF THE BRIDE CHEAT SHEET

Prewedding

- ☐ Host an engagement party (bride's family traditionally gets the first opportunity)
- ☐ Help couple decide on sites and/or make other big planning decisions
- ☐ Usually contributes to wedding budget
- ☐ Help bride put together family's guest list
- ☐ Offer suggestions for special family or ethnic ceremony traditions
- ☐ May help bride shop for her wedding gown
- ☐ Chooses own wedding-day outfit (may consult with mother of the groom about formality)
- ☐ Along with maid of honor and bridesmaids, may plan and host a shower
- ☐ On wedding day, help bride get ready
- ☐ May accompany daughter and husband to ceremony

At ceremony

- ☐ Are escorted by an usher (sometimes your son or husband) to your seat directly before the ceremony begins, if it's a Christian ceremony; in a Jewish ceremony, walk in procession with your daughter and husband and stand underneath huppah
- ☐ Walk in recessional with your husband if it's a Jewish wedding; in a Christian wedding, are escorted out after wedding party

At reception

- ☐ Greet guests in receiving line
- ☐ May be announced with your husband
- ☐ Sit in an honored place at parents' table
- ☐ May help coordinate vendors

Postwedding

- ☐ May host a post-wedding brunch

Other _____

_____

_____

_____

FATHER OF THE BRIDE CHEAT SHEET

Prewedding

- ☐ Along with your wife, host engagement party
- ☐ Contribute to the wedding budget
- ☐ Help couple decide on sites and/or make other big planning decisions
- ☐ May help choose hotel for out-of-town guests and reserve a block of reduced-rate rooms, create maps to be included with invitations, or anything else couple asks for help with
- ☐ Rent your own formalwear (talk with couple if you're to coordinate with wedding party)
- ☐ Help pick up out-of-town guests from the airport; may also arrange transportation to and from the wedding (vans, bus, and so on)
- ☐ Typically travel to ceremony with bride

At ceremony

- ☐ May escort your wife to her seat directly before a Christian ceremony begins; walk your daughter down the aisle in a Christian ceremony; in a Jewish wedding, walk with your daughter and wife and stand under huppah
- ☐ Walk in recessional with your wife in a Jewish wedding; in a Christian wedding, escort mother of the bride out after wedding party

At reception

- ☐ Greet guests in receiving line
- ☐ May be announced with your wife
- ☐ May make a welcoming speech
- ☐ Sit in an honored place at parents' table
- ☐ Toast the newlyweds after best man makes his speech and groom responds
- ☐ Do father-daughter dance with bride
- ☐ May take care of vendor balances at the end of the reception

Postwedding

- ☐ With wife, may host a postwedding brunch

Other _____

_____

_____

_____

Photocopy, cut out, and give to appropriate parties

MOTHER OF THE GROOM CHEAT SHEET

Prewedding

- ☐ Contact mother of the bride if the families are not acquainted (or plan a celebration even if you have met)
- ☐ Attend (first) engagement party if the bride's family hosts one
- ☐ Along with your husband, may host an additional engagement party for groom's side of the family
- ☐ Usually contribute to wedding budget
- ☐ May help couple decide on sites and/or make other big planning decisions
- ☐ Help groom put together family's guest list
- ☐ Offer suggestions for special family or ethnic ceremony traditions
- ☐ If you're close, may help bride shop for her wedding gown
- ☐ Choose your own wedding-day outfit (may consult with mother of the bride about formality)
- ☐ Along with your husband, plan and host the rehearsal dinner

At ceremony

- ☐ Are escorted by an usher (sometimes your son or husband) to your seat right before the mother of the bride is seated, if it's a Christian ceremony; in a Jewish ceremony, walk in procession with your son and husband and stand underneath huppah
- ☐ Walk in the recessional with your husband, if it's a Jewish wedding; in a Christian wedding, are escorted out after wedding party and bride's parents

At reception

- ☐ Greet guests in receiving line
- ☐ May be announced with her husband
- ☐ Sit in an honored place at parents' table
- ☐ Do mother-son dance with groom

Postwedding

- ☐ Attend or host postwedding brunch

Other _____

_____

FATHER OF THE GROOM CHEAT SHEET

Prewedding

- ☐ Attend (first) engagement party if the bride's family hosts one
- ☐ Along with your wife, may host an additional engagement party for groom's side of the family
- ☐ Along with wife, usually contribute to wedding budget
- ☐ May help couple decide on sites and/or make other big planning decisions
- ☐ Rent your own formalwear (after talking with couple if you're to be coordinated with the wedding party); attend fittings as needed
- ☐ Along with your wife, plan rehearsal dinner
- ☐ On wedding day, may travel to ceremony with the groom and best man

At ceremony

- ☐ May escort your wife to her seat (right before the mother of the bride is seated) and before the Christian ceremony begins; if it's a Jewish wedding, walk down the aisle with your son and wife and stand under huppah

- ☐ Walk in the recessional with your wife in a Jewish wedding; in a Christian wedding, escort mother of the groom out after wedding party and bride's parents

At reception

- ☐ Greet guests in receiving line
- ☐ May be announced with your wife
- ☐ May make a welcoming speech
- ☐ Sit in an honored place at parents' table
- ☐ May toast the newlyweds
- ☐ May settle final bills with wedding vendors

Postwedding

- ☐ Attend or host postwedding brunch

Other _____

_____

_____

_____

_____

_____

Photocopy, cut out, and give to appropriate parties

Family Issues

Q: What are our stepparents' wedding roles?

A: That's basically up to you and your families; it all depends on how comfortable everyone is about their participation. You may want to present stepparents with corsages or boutonnieres to mark their place in your families. If you're especially close to your stepmom, for example, you might ask her to do a reading during the ceremony or even take her place next to your dad in the receiving line. If there's a stepparent you or your fiancé(e) is not as close to, don't feel you have to go overboard if the feelings just aren't there; chances are the stepparent would feel just as awkward about having too big a role in your wedding as you would. Just be sure that no one is left feeling like an outsider. Talk to each parent separately about what he or she is comfortable with.

Q: How do we deal with ceremony and reception seating with divorced parents? What about the receiving line?

A: Traditionally, the parent who raised you sits in the front pew at the ceremony, and the other parent sits in the third pew (both with spouse, if remarried). The second pew serves as "breathing space" and also as seating for siblings and grandparents. If your parents don't like this arrangement and/or are on good terms, it's fine for everyone to sit in the front pew together, or in the first and second pews. At the reception, each parent, along with his or her spouse, should host a separate table of honored guests.

If you want both parents to stand in the receiving line, you must also decide whether to include stepparents. Keep your divorced parents separate—that is, don't put your mom next to your dad, lest people think they're still married. For example, if the bride's parents are divorced, her mom (and hubby) should stand in line in front of the bride and groom, then the groom's parents, and then the bride's dad (and stepmom, if applicable). A less logistically complicated solution is letting dads and stepdads circulate among the guests while the moms and you do the receiving line. The bottom line: Whatever is the most comfortable and the least confusing for everyone is the thing to do.

Q: My mother passed away last year. Any ideas for honoring her at the wedding?

A: There are plenty of wonderful and appropriate ways to honor a parent who's passed away. The one thing you don't want to do is mention her on the invitation; the parents listed there are the hosts of the wedding. Here are some other options.

- Include a written tribute to Mom in your program.
- Include a moment of silence in the ceremony or light a candle.
- Have someone read her favorite passage from scripture or sing her favorite song.
- Place a flower from your bouquet on the empty seat next to your dad.
- Carry or wear something of hers.
- Talk about and toast her at the reception.
- Visit her grave postceremony and leave your bouquet.

Q: I was raised by my stepfather, but I have recently become close to my biological dad. Who should walk me down the aisle?

A: There are multiple solutions for this dilemma, which is becoming more and more common. Consider walking with both of them—walk in with your dad, and then meet your stepfather halfway and walk up to the altar with him, since he raised you. Another option: Choose one to walk you down the aisle and ask the other to take an honored role in the ceremony by doing a reading or holding the huppah, for example. Or ask your mom to be your aisle escort, or even do the aisle walk yourself, and dance with both dads at the reception. Be sure to talk it over with each of them before you come to a decision.

Knot Knowledge: Attendants

Ask ASAP Don't wait too long to invite your nearest and dearest to be in your wedding. You don't want them wondering whether you're going to ask them or not—or worse, assuming they're in your wedding when they're not!

Don't Diss Distance Don't automatically rule out friends or siblings who live far away. Your attendants are more than people to help you plan your wedding.

Skip the Symmetry You don't need the same number of attendants on each side; if the bride wants five maids and the groom has only three guys in mind, that's fine.

Kids Are Optional If there are no children you two feel particularly close to, you don't need a flower girl and/or ring bearer.

Don't Assume When they agree to be in the wedding, make sure each attendant is aware of his or her responsibilities—financial and planning-wise.

Be Reasonable Keep in mind that even local attendants have their own lives; it's not fair to expect them to drop everything every time you have a wedding crisis.

How "Special" Is That Role, Really? If you're feeling bad about not being able to include someone as an attendant, think twice before offering them a position such as guest-book watcher. Would you want to do that? They'll be happier with a corsage.

Don't Want a Wedding Party? You don't need attendants—you just need two witnesses over the age of twenty-one to sign your marriage license after the ceremony.

Knot Knowledge: Parents

Easy Money? Don't simply assume your parents are going to write a huge check and then leave you to your own devices. Be (or at least act) grateful for any financial help you receive.

Do Your Research Before you sit down with your families to talk money, find out how much wedding services typically cost in your town (ballpark figures are fine), so you'll have a starting point.

Ask Their Opinion They might actually have something helpful to say. Ask them what they think about potential wedding sites, florists, cake flavors, whatever.

Give Them Something to Do Even if you want to plan the wedding mostly yourself, you'll want your parents to feel useful (especially your moms—that's their job). Put them in charge of duties they're interested in and excited about—but that you don't feel the need to control yourself.

Get the Dads in on It Legend has it that dads do nothing but pull out their credit cards during wedding planning. Try to make yours feel a bit more important than that!

Be Sensitive to Steps There's nothing like a wedding to bring out insecurity in stepparents and actual parents alike. Try to make everyone feel involved, but draw the line at ultimatums ("If that woman's invited, I'm not going").

Let Them Plan Their Own Parties As much as you might want to tell your mom how to plan your shower or nudge the groom's parents in the "right" direction about the rehearsal dinner, resist. Concentrate on wedding planning.

Best Friends from Birth? Moms can absolutely be matrons of honor; dads make fantastic best men.

Be Sure to Thank Them Give your parents gifts of gratitude soon before the wedding—yes, they know you love and appreciate them, but it never hurts to remind them how much.

Knot Knowledge: Guests

Keep Them Posted If many of your guests are out-of-towners, send out a few mailings after your save-the-date letter; you might want to send (or e-mail) periodic updates, with hotel information, wedding activities, and the like.

Make a Wedding Web Page Keep guests informed by creating a Web page where they can look up details about your wedding (directions, accommodations, and other details) at any time, day or night. Visit **www.TheKnot.com** to do so.

Put Them Up Reserve a block of rooms at a hotel or bed-and-breakfast close to the wedding sites. Research airfares and car-rental companies. Let guests know about any deals you find.

Welcome Them Welcome baskets in each room are a great way to say, "Hey, glad you're here!" Include fruit, cheese, chocolates, bottled water, and other goodies. Also include directions (maps) to the ceremony and reception sites.

That's Entertainment If guests will be in town for several days, give them ideas for things to do—perhaps a list of your favorite restaurants, shops, and museums, plus maps and tourist brochures.

Put Them in Touch Leave a list of all guests staying in the hotel (add in room numbers at the last minute), plus local contact information (parents, you two, local attendants).

Ask for Hosting Help Attendants or local friends can organize a sight-seeing trip, a barbecue, or a pizza party for out-of-towners. (You don't have to be at every event, but make an appearance if possible.)

Be Seated Don't wait until the last minute to draw up a seating chart. Do it at least a week before the wedding. You can always make last-minute changes, but you don't want to have to deal with the whole thing the night before.

Show Your Love During the reception, toast out-of-town guests.

Guest Etiquette

Q: We're having a small wedding. Do we have to include "and guest" on single people's invitations? If we don't, what if someone replies for two anyway?

A: Most guests understand that without "and guest" or another name on the invitation, it's meant for them alone. If you're having a small wedding, you probably aren't going to be able to invite everyone with a date, unless it's a fiancé(e) and/or a serious significant other. (Technically, you're never supposed to use "and guest"; instead, you should find out the name of the date, but you've probably seen "and guest" a lot anyway, because it's easier than asking everyone whom they're planning to bring.) What to do if a clueless soul replies for two? Call and explain that you're having an intimate wedding and were not able to invite everyone with a guest.

Q: Are out-of-towners supposed to be invited to the rehearsal dinner?

A: A rehearsal dinner can be as simple as the couple, their immediate families, and the wedding party plus their spouses or significant others. Or you can make it a bash and invite all your out-of-town guests. It's a very good opportunity to spend some time with visiting friends and relatives—you'll be more relaxed than at the wedding, and you'll probably be able to chat with people you might not get a chance to really sit down with later. If you want to maximize your quality time with those out-of-towners, invite 'em all to the rehearsal dinner. If you decide not to, don't leave them hanging—be sure some sort of party or event is planned for them, or that they can entertain themselves.

Q: Can I invite guests to the ceremony but not the reception?

A: Avoid this if at all possible. People may feel bad if you invite them to view the wedding but then don't include them in the celebration afterward; they may even suspect you did it only to get a gift! The one exception: If you are active in your church or temple, you may want to extend an open invitation to the ceremony to the entire congregation.

What about inviting guests to the reception but not the ceremony? It's okay to do this if you have your heart set on a superintimate, family-only vow exchange but want to party with all your friends and loved ones afterward.

Q: If we're asking guests to travel and stay overnight, do we have to pay their way?

A: You're not responsible for your guests' airfare or overnight costs, and most people are well aware of this fact. What you can do is recommend places for them to stay. Many hotels offer a discounted group rate if you book a certain number of rooms for your wedding. If certain must-have-there guests can't afford to stay in a hotel, try to arrange for them to stay with local bridesmaids, groomsmen, relatives, or friends (preferably people they already know). Don't invite out-of-towners to stay with you (unless it's your maid of honor we're talking about). You'll have enough stress already!

CONTACT CHEAT SHEET: Key Family & Attendants

Bride's parents: _____   Arrival: ____/____/____

Address: _____   Phone: _____

_____   E-mail: _____

Bride's parents II: _____   Arrival: ____/____/____

Address: _____   Phone: _____

_____   E-mail: _____

Groom's parents: _____   Arrival: ____/____/____

Address: _____   Phone: _____

_____   E-mail: _____

Groom's parents II: _____   Arrival: ____/____/____

Address: _____   Phone: _____

_____   E-mail: _____

Honor attendant: _____   Arrival: ____/____/____

Address: _____   Phone: _____

_____   E-mail: _____

Honor attendant: _____   Arrival: ____/____/____

Address: _____   Phone: _____

_____   E-mail: _____

CONTACT CHEAT SHEET: Bride's Attendants

Attendant: _____   Arrival: ____/____/____
Address: _____   Phone: _____
_____   E-mail: _____

Attendant: _____   Arrival: ____/____/____
Address: _____   Phone: _____
_____   E-mail: _____

Attendant: _____   Arrival: ____/____/____
Address: _____   Phone: _____
_____   E-mail: _____

Attendant: _____   Arrival: ____/____/____
Address: _____   Phone: _____
_____   E-mail: _____

Attendant: _____   Arrival: ____/____/____
Address: _____   Phone: _____
_____   E-mail: _____

Attendant: _____   Arrival: ____/____/____
Address: _____   Phone: _____
_____   E-mail: _____

Attendant: _____   Arrival: ____/____/____
Address: _____   Phone: _____
_____   E-mail: _____

CONTACT CHEAT SHEET: Groom's Attendants

Attendant: _____   Arrival: _____/_____/_____

Address: _____   Phone: _____

_____   E-mail: _____

Attendant: _____   Arrival: _____/_____/_____

Address: _____   Phone: _____

_____   E-mail: _____

Attendant: _____   Arrival: _____/_____/_____

Address: _____   Phone: _____

_____   E-mail: _____

Attendant: _____   Arrival: _____/_____/_____

Address: _____   Phone: _____

_____   E-mail: _____

Attendant: _____   Arrival: _____/_____/_____

Address: _____   Phone: _____

_____   E-mail: _____

Attendant: _____   Arrival: _____/_____/_____

Address: _____   Phone: _____

_____   E-mail: _____

Attendant: _____   Arrival: _____/_____/_____

Address: _____   Phone: _____

_____   E-mail: _____

CONTACT CHEAT SHEET: Guests' Hotels

Hotel: _____   Guests: _____

Address: _____   _____

_____   _____

Contact: _____   _____

Phone: _____   _____

Fax: _____   _____

Number of rooms in block reserved: _____   _____

Reserved under name: _____   _____

Group rate: $_____/night   _____

Hotel: _____   Guests: _____

Address: _____   _____

_____   _____

Contact: _____   _____

Phone: _____   _____

Fax: _____   _____

Number of rooms in block reserved: _____   _____

Reserved under name: _____   _____

Group rate: $_____/night   _____

Addresses or Web sites for local points of interest

_____

_____

_____

Notes

_____

_____

_____

_____

HATSHEPSUT & RICHARD: ADDING AFRICAN HERITAGE, CARIBBEAN CULTURE, AND EGYPTIAN RELIGION

August 24

Duxbury, Massachusetts

Planning Time Frame: One Year

HATSHEPSUT AND RICHARD wed in a festive and warm cultural celebration at Blairhaven Retreat Center. Their wedding embraced their African heritage, their Caribbean culture, and their practice of ancient Egyptian religion—the Kemmetic teachings of the Husea.

The bride marched into the wedding accompanied by both her parents, because in the Kemmetic tradition, there must be representation of a balance of male and female energy. Behind the trio, one of her attendants carried a 5-foot-tall parasol over the bride's head, since in the Ghanaian tradition, royalty always walked protected under parasols.

Honoring the Yoruba and Ghanaian traditions of the couples' ancestors, they chose to display various protective elements on a table by the altar, including salt (for sustaining life), water (to purify their bodies), a shield (to protect the home), and a broom (to remember to keep order in the house)—which they jumped over as their officiant pronounced them husband and wife.

Personalizing Elements

- THE ATTIRE. The rich, warm colors chosen for the wedding (yellow, turquoise, coral, and brown) are the primary colors representing Oshun, the spiritual guardian of love and beauty. Hatshepsut, a jewelry designer, chose a two-piece yellow ensemble with matching wrap and lots of intricate pieces of gold jewelry that she

made herself. Her bridesmaids wore rich, deep orange silk shantung dresses with deep orange silk organza overlays; the maid and matron of honor were dressed similarly in turquoise.

- THE FLOWERS. Each attendant carried a palm fan (in lieu of a more traditional bouquet of blooms) signifying the many practical uses of palm in Caribbean cultures.

- THE MUSIC. Music is important to the couple (he's a performing arts physical therapist), so they hired a steel pannist, who played calypso music as the guests arrived, and reggae during the ceremony. "Calypso was primarily used as social commentary throughout the Caribbean," explains Hatshepsut. The bride marched into the wedding to Bob Marley's "This Love That I'm Feeling." At the close of the ceremony, the pannist began to celebrate the union with his rendition of Bob Marley's "One Love."

- THE CAKE. As part of the large Jamaican-African feast that followed the ceremony, guests enjoyed a signature rum punch and a traditional Caribbean black cake (a rum cake) that was adorned in candy cowry shells, which, in Africa, are used as symbols of prosperity.

ceremony

We start with the ceremony because it *is* your wedding. For some, a favorite family officiant or house of worship drives all the choices regarding the ceremony. For others, it's
built around a beloved location. Be aware in advance that if you want a religious service, there are
rules involved—not just about where the ceremony takes place and how it's structured, but also
about the words, music, people, and rituals involved. Make sure to okay everything with your
priest, minister, or rabbi. If you'll have a civil (secular) ceremony, feel free to be as creative as you
like. If your ceremony will be at your reception site, you'll still want to use the following worksheet
as it relates to officiants and ceremony organization.

Ceremony Style Worksheet

Ceremony
- ☐ Religious
- ☐ Long and symbolic (e.g., full Mass)
- ☐ Civil (secular)
- ☐ Short and sweet (just vows)

Religion(s) _____

Location
- ☐ In house of worship
- ☐ Indoors
- ☐ In secular space
- ☐ Outdoors

Guests
- ☐ Just couple and family
- ☐ All reception guests

Attendants # for bride: _____   # for groom: _____

Rituals (check all that apply and add those from your own religion)
- ☐ Vow exchange (traditional or original vows?)
- ☐ Ring exchange
- ☐ Readings
- ☐ Unity ritual (candle)
- ☐ Marriage contract
- ☐ Moment of silence
- ☐ Offering to ancestors
- ☐ Performance
- ☐ Wine-sharing ritual

Jewish rituals
- ☐ Ketubah
- ☐ B'deken (veiling of the bride)
- ☐ Sheva brachot (seven blessings)
- ☐ Breaking the glass
- ☐ Huppah (wedding canopy)
- ☐ Tish
- ☐ Kiddushin
- ☐ Yichud

Remarriage (with children) rituals
- ☐ Family vow exchange
- ☐ Family unity ritual (candle or other)
- ☐ Exchange of ring (or medallion) between new parent and child

Other rituals or requirements of your culture or religion

_____

_____

Vow or reading ideas (separate from rituals)

_____

_____

Ceremony budget $_____

Calling All Ceremony Sites & Officiants

First you need to find a ceremony site. Religious options include notable local churches, your current church or temple, your parents' church or synagogue, a house of worship you're interested in joining as a married couple, a military chapel (if one or both of you is in the service), or a college chapel (at your alma mater). For civil sites, the sky's the limit.

Find an officiant if your site is not a house of worship. For a civil wedding, contact city, town, or village halls and ask about judges or justices of the peace available for weddings. If you have no connection to a specific church but want an officiant of a certain denomination to perform your ceremony, ask friends and/or search for one online at **www.TheKnot.com/local** for names of churches and synagogues. Try nondenominational or interfaith officiants. (These officiants will perform ceremonies at nonreligious sites.)

Make appointments with several sites and/or officiants (unless you're marrying in your own house of worship and the decision is a given):

Location: _____   Location: _____

Address: _____   Address: _____

Officiant: _____   Officiant: _____

Phone: _____   Phone: _____

Fee: _____   Fee: _____

App't date: ___ /___/___ Time: _____   App't date: ___ /___/___ Time: _____

Available dates: ___ /___/___ ___ /___/___   Available dates: ___ /___/___ ___ /___/___

Notes: _____   Notes: _____

_____   _____

_____   _____

Officiant: _____   Officiant: _____

Phone: _____   Phone: _____

Fee: _____   Fee: _____

App't date: ___ /___/___ Time: _____   App't date: ___ /___/___ Time: _____

Available dates: ___ /___/___ ___ /___/___   Available dates: ___ /___/___ ___ /___/___

Notes: _____   Notes: _____

_____   _____

_____   _____

Questions to Ask Site Managers & Officiants

☐ Is the site/officiant available on your preferred wedding date?

☐ Does the site/officiant charge a standard fee? Is it a donation to the house of worship, a fee to rent the space, a specific amount paid to the officiant?

☐ If you want to marry at a nonreligious site, is a religious officiant willing to marry you there?

☐ Is the sanctuary or other ceremony space large enough for the approximate number of guests you're planning to invite? Where will everyone (the wedding party, the officiant, you two, musicians) stand? Do you like the setup?

☐ What will the site supply (prayer books, aisle runner, huppah, wine goblets, candelabra, yarmulkes, and so on)?

☐ Are there any restrictions on how you can decorate the sanctuary or ceremony area? What about rules for photography or videography?

☐ Are there restrictions on music?

☐ Are there any restrictions on attire? (Some churches require shoulders to be covered; if your dress is sleeveless, you'll want a shawl or other cover-up.)

☐ Must you use the site's in-house musicians, or can you bring in your own? Is there an additional fee?

☐ If your ceremony will be outdoors in a public place, do you need a permit? When/where should you apply? Are there restrictions (number of people gathered, for example)?

☐ If you prefer a small ceremony, will the officiant marry you in his or her study or chambers, or is there a small chapel off the main sanctuary that you can use?

☐ Can you write original vows, or does the officiant use standard ceremony wording? If so, can it be modified to suit your ceremony?

☐ Do you choose the readings, or do you pick from a list of readings the house of worship/officiant has selected?

☐ Is prewedding counseling required? Is it one-on-one with your officiant, or in a group setting with other couples? How many sessions?

☐ Will the officiant be your primary contact at the wedding site, or is there an on-site wedding consultant, sexton, or someone else?

☐ Will the officiant be available for a ceremony rehearsal?

☐ Ask yourself: Does the officiant make you comfortable? Does he or she seem genuinely interested in you as a couple? Be sure you like and respect your officiant—and that the feelings are reciprocated.

Ceremony Etiquette & Issues

Q: We are of different faiths. What do we do about an officiant?

A: An interfaith ceremony may take a bit more planning, creativity, and communication than if the two of you were the same religion. Be forewarned: One of you may be asked to convert or be baptized, so get the details as soon as possible. The best way to blend the traditions of your faiths is to choose co-officiants. Officiants of most Christian denominations are supportive of interfaith marriage (although it may be difficult to find a willing Catholic priest), and more and more Reform rabbis are willing to co-officiate as well (Orthodox or Conservative rabbis may decline). If you can't find two officiants, look for one who's open to including traditions from both religions in the ceremony. Another option is to have a secular ceremony now, then renew your vows in your church and/or your fiancé(e)'s temple later.

Q: Is it possible to bring our own officiant into a church we choose?

A: If you wish to marry in a specific church, it's proper to ask the minister or pastor there to officiate at your wedding ceremony. If you want someone else to officiate, discuss this with the minister; traditionally it is he or she who should invite the other officiant. This is etiquette, but it's also common sense; you can't *tell* the pastor of a church that you are bringing someone else in. You can only ask if it's a possibility; and find out the best way to go about it. If you're set on the other officiant, your best bet may be to work with him or her to settle on another site.

Q: How can we include our children from previous marriages in our ceremony?

A: Depending on how old they are, your kids could be included in the wedding party as attendants, junior attendants, or flower girls and ring bearers. Or they might like to do a reading during the ceremony. Children can escort the bride (their mother) down the aisle, symbolically giving her their blessing. No matter how you decide to involve them, consider a special family vow exchange, prayer, or reading directly after you exchange marriage vows, in which you each promise to love and care for your spouse's children, reinforcing your new family ties. Some couples also present their kids with gifts—jewelry for girls, watches for boys, for instance—to commemorate the day and their important role in it. Ask your kids what they'd like to do, and don't insist they participate if they're uncomfortable about it.

Q: How does the unity candle ritual work?

A: Many couples include in the ceremony a ritual symbolic of the joining of their lives. The unity candle is usually a large column with two thinner tapers on either side of it; the thinner candles are lit either before the ceremony begins or by your mothers before the ritual is to take place. After your vows, you each take one of the smaller, lit candles (which represent your two families and/or your individual lives) and light the middle candle together. Variations: You can use two cups of wine, poured by representatives from each family and the two of you pour wine from each into a third cup and then drink from it. There's also the "vessel and rose," a relatively new tradition in which the groom presents the bride with a rose and she gives him a vase to hold it. There's also a Native American tradition that blends different-colored sands to represent unity. Feel free to get creative and make up your own ritual.

What It Costs Fees can vary from none or a moderate donation to upward of $1,000 for high-demand, big-city cathedrals. This fee may be separate from the officiant's fee, which can run from $150 to $800. Fees may be considered a (tax-deductible) donation to the site if it's a house of worship. Every site is different; ask up front. If your ceremony musicians are in-house staff, their fee may be included in your location cost. If not, plan to spend between $50 and $350 per hour for a minimum of two hours of work.

Ways to Save Have your ceremony in a special spot at your reception location (but if you're having a religious officiant, check to make sure this is okay). Marry in your own church or temple. Don't choose the National Cathedral (popular places suggest larger donations). Stick to a smaller chapel, instead of the pricier main sanctuary. Choose a public site such as a park. Visit city hall.

Holiday Hot Spots Certain times of year may be off-limits for weddings in particular religions—for example, the High Holidays in Judaism. Also, you may not be able to wed during Lent in the Greek Orthodox or Roman Catholic Church.

Consider Religious Requirements If you choose to have a religious ceremony, be prepared to comply with all the rules and beliefs that go along with it. If you find that you can't do so because of your own beliefs, you may want to reconsider and wed at a nonreligious site, where you'll have more input.

Keep Vows Simple If you write your own vows, keep them relatively short and personal (but not *too* personal), and decide ahead of time if you'll memorize them or carry a written version down the aisle. You don't want to forget your lines!

Make a Program Ceremony programs aren't required, but they're a great place to list and thank your wedding party and close family. If you're including special religious or ethnic traditions guests may not understand, a program is a perfect way to explain them. Include words to special readings or songs.

Proceed Without Caution Don't worry too much about processional and recessional order; during your ceremony rehearsal, your officiant will make sure everyone knows where to stand, when to walk, and when to sit.

Invite Your Officiant Send your officiant and his or her spouse an invitation to your reception; plan to seat them with your parents or another family table. Especially if your officiant has known your family for a long time, you'll definitely want him or her there. Many officiants decline (they may have another wedding to preside at), but they'll appreciate the gesture.

Pay Their Way If your officiant is coming from a distance to perform your ceremony, it's appropriate for you to offer to cover the costs of travel and accommodations.

Booking the Ceremony Site Checklist

☐ Choose your site and officiant and confirm in writing; include your wedding date and time.

☐ If you'll need to rent anything, contact a rental company (your florist may be able to supply some of the following):
    ☐ Ceremony chairs #_____
    ☐ Huppah
    ☐ Columns or arch to delineate the place where you'll say your vows
    ☐ Candelabra
    ☐ Wire stands for flowers

☐ Research ceremony readings and religious or ethnic ceremony customs or traditions; set up a second meeting to discuss these with your officiant.

☐ Ask officiant for a copy of his or her standard ceremony so that you can make changes to suit you (if allowed).

☐ If prewedding counseling is required, schedule and go:

Date(s) and time(s) to meet with officiant: _____

_____

Date(s) and other pertinent info about group meetings and/or weekends away:

_____

_____

_____

☐ Finalize overall structure and elements of ceremony (readings, lighting candles, special rituals) as well as who will participate in each.

☐ Determine which of the following ceremony items you will need; start shopping or make arrangements to have them made:
    ☐ Ketubah or other marriage contract (e.g., Quaker)
    ☐ Yarmulkes
    ☐ Unity candle
    ☐ Aisle runner
    ☐ Ring pillow
    ☐ Other elements (crowns for a Greek Orthodox ceremony, broom for an Afrocentric ceremony)

    _____

    _____

☐ If you'll write your own vows, start working on them together at least two months before the wedding; consult your officiant if you need help.

To-Do List: Wedding Rings

Material   ☐ White gold   ☐ Platinum
                ☐ Yellow gold   ☐ Silver

Style   ☐ Embedded gems   ☐ Plain band
                ☐ Ornate   ☐ Custom-designed
                ☐ Fitted to engagement ring   ☐ Ready-made
                ☐ Different for bride and groom   ☐ Identical

☐ Ring budget:

     Total: $_____ (Groom $_____ Bride $_____)

☐ Ring sizes: Groom _____ Bride _____

☐ Inscriptions to be engraved:

     Bride: _____

     Groom: _____

☐ Research reputable jewelers (try **www.theknot.com/jewelers**)

☐ Choose a jeweler:

     Store: _____

     Contact: _____

     Address: _____

     Phone: _____

     Referred by: _____

     Notes: _____

     _____

     _____

☐ Order your rings

     Date ordered: _____ / _____ / _____   Deposit: $_____

     Date ready: _____ / _____ / _____   Balance: $_____

☐ Review inscriptions before you leave the store.

To-Do List: Marriage License

☐ Find the marriage license bureau in the city or town *where you will marry*. (In the United States, look in the blue government section of the local white pages under "Marriage," or check online.) Phone: _____

☐ Call the marriage license bureau and ask:

Address: _____

Hours: _____ Best time to come: _____

- Do you need blood tests to marry in that state? ☐ Y ☐ N
- When must you apply? Within _____ weeks of wedding
- Which of the following must you bring with you?
  ☐ Certified copies of your birth certificates
  ☐ Proof of citizenship
  ☐ Government-issue photo ID (driver's license or passport)
  ☐ Blood test results (if required)
  ☐ Parental consent (if underage)
  ☐ Death certificate (if widowed)
  ☐ Divorce decree (if divorced)
- How much will the license cost? $_____
- Payment options? ☐ check   ☐ credit card   ☐ cash

☐ Make appointments to get blood tests (if required)

Where: _____

Address: _____

Contact: _____

Date: _____ / _____ / _____ Time: _____

Cost: $_____ Payment options? ☐ check   ☐ credit card   ☐ cash

☐ Pick up test results:

Date: _____ / _____ / _____

☐ Go in person (both of you) to apply for your license. Exactly when you go depends on the window of time (around your wedding date) that a license is valid in your state; it will probably be two or three weeks before.

☐ Give your marriage license to your officiant prior to or on your wedding day. He will sign it and file it with the proper office. A copy will be sent to you in a couple of weeks.

☐ File your license in a safe place.

ROBIN & ADAM:
A JEWISH CELEBRATION

June 14
Montauk, NY
Planning Time Frame: 8 Months

ROBIN AND ADAM'S Middle-Eastern Jewish wedding was a celebration of their heritage. "It was a very powerful feeling to go through these rituals that are thousands of years old," Robin says. "We felt tied to one another as well as our history."

An artist painted pomegranate branches—symbolic of love, prosperity, and fertility in Judaism—on the couple's *ketubah* (wedding certificate) and invitation. Lebanese wedding-dress designer Reem Acra designed the bride a square-necked gown of ivory and gold—traditional Persian-Jewish wedding-dress colors—with embroidery based on an antique Turkish design. Henna artists spent four hours painting Robin's arms, hands, feet, and ankles at a traditional henna party for all the women involved in the wedding. On the Saturday night before the wedding, Robin performed a *mikvah,* or ritual immersion in the freezing cold Atlantic ocean.

The ceremony was held under a *huppah* brought from Israel by a friend of the bride. First was the *tisch*—the teaching from the Torah—which Robin and Adam, untraditionally, did together. During the procession, the musicians performed a Sephardic wedding song in the original Ladino, a mixture of Hebrew and Spanish. In lieu of vows, Robin and Adam read their ketubah. At the end of the ceremony, in the Sephardic tradition, the couple's

mothers wrapped them in a tallis, literally binding them together.

After a traditional *yichud*—during which the couple spent time alone together directly after the ceremony—it was on to the reception, where guests enjoyed a feast of olives, hummus, kabobs, tomato and cucumber salad, pita, and couscous. The caterer also made a special dish called *sutlach,* a sweet rice pudding that is a traditional first course at Sephardic Jewish weddings. After guests grooved to an R&B band, an avant-garde klezmer band played traditional Jewish wedding music with a twist.

Robin and Adam's New Jewish Wedding Tips

- "Do some research. We read a great deal, not just about weddings, but also Jewish perspectives on love and marriage." A book that Robin and Adam highly recommend is *The New Jewish Wedding,* by Anita Diamant (Summit Books, 1996).
- "Customize. It's important to adapt and reinterpret traditions. We didn't want to do anything just because we had to. There was not a single element of our wedding that Adam and I didn't put ourselves into."

CONTACT CHEAT SHEET:
Site & Officiant

Site: _____

Address: _____

_____

Contact: _____

Phone: _____

Fax: _____

E-mail: _____

Officiant name: _____

Phone (if different from site contact): _____

Room(s) and time reserved (if applicable): _____

_____

Donation or fee for ceremony site: $_____

Donation or fee for officiant: $_____

Name of organization check for donation should be made out to: _____

_____

Total cost $_____

Deposit $_____   Date paid: ____ / ____ / ____

Balance $_____   Date due: ____ / ____ / ____

Notes

_____

_____

_____

_____

_____

_____

_____

_____

_____

_____

staple business card here

Notes

CHAPTER FIVE

reception site

Find your location fast. Your choice will define your wedding style and dictate most of your other planning decisions. Try to book at least a year in advance—for the most popular places, a year and a half (or even two years) is not too early. Also make sure you have a good idea of the head count before you begin looking; a site for fifty is completely different from one for five hundred. If your caterer comes with your reception site, make sure to consult the checklists in Chapter 7 before you make any final decisions.

Reception Site Worksheet

Before you start pounding the pavement, check the box(es) under each heading that best describe your image of your wedding location. It will give your search some focus.

Uses (check all that apply)
- ☐ Ceremony
- ☐ Dressing
- ☐ Reception
- ☐ Dancing

Services
- ☐ All-inclusive (site and food)
- ☐ Do-it-yourself clean slate
- ☐ Rentals (chairs, linens, cake table, etc.) included

Location
- ☐ Walking distance from ceremony
- ☐ Near ceremony site (within ___ minutes)
- ☐ Indoors
- ☐ Outdoors
- ☐ Indoor/outdoor

Features
- ☐ Best in evening
- ☐ Breathtaking interiors
- ☐ By the water
- ☐ Outdoors, under tent
- ☐ Best in daylight
- ☐ Breathtaking views
- ☐ In nature

Style
- ☐ Old-world, ornate
- ☐ Modern, spare
- ☐ Formal
- ☐ Big and grand
- ☐ Rustic
- ☐ Fun, funky
- ☐ Casual
- ☐ Intimate

Special requirements
- ☐ Disabled access
- ☐ Coat check
- ☐ Separate children's room
- ☐ Parking

Other: _____

_____

Size
Must accommodate: #_____ guests

Reception site budget $_____

Calling All Reception Sites

To find sites, research hotels, resorts, bed-and-breakfasts, inns, country clubs, banquet halls, historic mansions, notable buildings, local attractions (private gardens, vineyards, orchards, zoos, museums, aquariums, train stations), civic buildings (community centers, town halls), lofts, art galleries, studios, rooftop gardens, military academics or bases, college campus buildings, city parks, state beaches, cruise ships, yachts, a favorite restaurant, a ranch, or your home or backyard. Also log onto **www.TheKnot.com/local** to find hundreds of sites in your city.

Make appointments to see several sites:

Location: _____   Location: _____

Address: _____   Address: _____

Phone: _____   Phone: _____

Web site: _____   Web site: _____

Manager: _____   Manager: _____

App't date: ___ /___/___ Time: _____   App't date: ___ /___/___ Time: _____

Rental estimate: $_____   Rental estimate: $_____

Per-head costs: $ _____ – $ _____   Per-head costs: $ _____ – $ _____

Notes: _____   Notes: _____

_____   _____

_____   _____

Location: _____   Location: _____

Address: _____   Address: _____

Phone: _____   Phone: _____

Web site: _____   Web site: _____

Manager: _____   Manager: _____

App't date: ___ /___/___ Time: _____   App't date: ___ /___/___ Time: _____

Rental estimate: $_____   Rental estimate: $_____

Per-head costs: $ _____ – $ _____   Per-head costs: $ _____ – $ _____

Notes: _____   Notes: _____

_____   _____

_____   _____

Questions to Ask Reception Site Managers

☐ Is the site available on your date (or a date acceptable to you)?

☐ For how many hours will you have the site? Are there overtime fees?

☐ How does the place charge—per head, by the hour, or flat fee?

☐ Can you bring in your own caterer, florist, and so on, or must you use in-house staff? (Determine if food service is included in your location contract; see Chapter 7 for more catering questions.)

☐ Does the site have a liquor license? Can you bring in your own alcohol?

☐ Can you see sample floor plans and/or visit when the room is set up for a wedding? Where does the band usually set up, buffet usually go, and so on?

☐ What's the staff-guest ratio? (Use your common sense here—one or two waiters can't manage a party of two hundred.)

☐ How many people will the space comfortably hold (not just official capacity, which may not consider space for tables, musical equipment, and such)?

☐ What will/can the facility provide?
  ☐ Cooking facilities   ☐ Tables   ☐ Chairs
  ☐ Dinnerware   ☐ Linens   ☐ Tent
  ☐ Additional lighting   ☐ Dance floor   ☐ _____

☐ Does the room have adequate outlets (and power) for food-preparation equipment, lighting, and audio needs?

☐ Is there adequate lighting? Who will control the lighting during the reception?

☐ Is there a dance floor, or must one be brought in? Can the site arrange it, or are you responsible for renting one? Is there an additional fee?

☐ Are there any restrictions or rules about entertainment, decorations, and such? What about dress code?

☐ Are the bathrooms clean? Are there attendants? Do you need to tip them?

☐ Is there ample parking? Are there attendants (and do you need to tip them)?

☐ If necessary, is there good security (and do you need to tip security people, or even bring them in yourselves)?

☐ Will there be other weddings on the same day or at the same time?

☐ Will the manager be present to oversee your reception to the end?

☐ Can you get references of couples who had their weddings at the site?

☐ Ask yourself: Is the manager flexible and willing to accommodate you?

☐ Does the site have liability insurance?

Reception Etiquette

Q: What happens when at a reception?

A: Draw up your own schedule based on this general time line:
1. Cocktails are served outside the main reception room.
2. Wedding party arrives and receiving line forms.
3. Everyone moves into the main room (after picking up place cards) and is seated.
4. The MC (best man, bandleader or bride and groom) welcomes everyone.
5. The first dance may happen now.
6. First course is served, or guests start going up to the buffet. (If it's a cocktail or dessert reception, toasts begin.)
7. Toasts happen as guests are finishing their salad course or entrée.
8. Dancing begins with the first dance.
9. Couple's toast.
10. The couple cuts the cake; cake is served.
11. Bouquet and garter tosses (optional).
12. Dancing continues until the party winds down.
13. Last dance.

Q: Do we have to do a receiving line? How does it work?

A: I like receiving lines because they ensure that you'll spend one-on-one time with each and every guest on your wedding day. It's customary to have one if you've invited fifty guests or more, but if you're having a hundred or more, it's a must. The line can form casually at the ceremony site after the wedding (as people are leaving) or at the reception site as guests are arriving. Pick a spot (ahead of time) where there is room for people to form a line while they wait. Many couples include their parents—the bride's parents are first, then the bride and groom, then the groom's parents—or it can be just the two of you. Don't think of it as an annoying formality; you are simply standing still to facilitate all the hugs and handshakes.

Q: Who toasts, when, and in what order?

A: Toasting is the fastest-growing reception trend. It may begin before the reception meal is served, or between courses. Traditionally, the best man serves as master of ceremonies (you know, the famous best-man speech), toasting his pal and his new wife. The groom responds, thanking his family, the bride's family, and the guests, and finally toasting his bride. These days, the bride and groom often toast together. Often the maid of honor also makes a speech, and friends and family take the mike throughout the evening to tell stories and offer good wishes in marathon toasting sessions. Make it clear to your DJ, bandleader, or MC if you want people to be able to toast at will or not.

Q: What's the best way to find a good party-rental company?

A: Check online at **www.TheKnot.com/local** for rental companies. It's a good idea to call the American Rental Association at 800-334-2177 (**www.ararental.org**) as well—cross-reference your list with local referrals from that national organization. When you visit a rental agent, supply this information: date, time, and location of your wedding; approximate size of your guest list; size and formality of the celebration; style or theme, if any; and any site specifics that will affect what you can rent or where you can put things. As with any wedding vendor, you'll want to draw up a contract or letter of agreement with your rental company.

Knot Knowledge: Reception Site Tips

What It Costs Most sites that include catering charge by guest, from $10 to $200 or more per head, depending on formality (of the party and the place), type of meal, and locale (city vs. rural area, East or West Coast vs. Midwest). Flat fees for sites you are renting purely as locations can range from $1,000 to $10,000 or more.

Ways to Save Marry in a month other than June, August, September, or October. Stay away from Saturday night—opt for a Thursday, Friday, or Sunday. Take advantage of your country-club membership or alumni status, or choose a city- or state-run site such as a public park or historic building. See page 74 for ways to save on per-head costs.

The Cooler, the More Complicated If you choose a creative location such as a light-house or art gallery—or any location that doesn't do a lot of weddings—there will be more details to work out than if you choose a place that's known for wedding celebrations and has a planning brigade already in place.

Pay for Privacy If there will be other parties going on at your site at the same time as yours, you'll want to be sure it's not possible to hear music coming from other rooms, and that there are enough bathrooms, coatrooms, and other facilities, so things won't feel cramped. Ask if you can check things out at a time when several parties are taking place. (Keep in mind, though, that privacy can cost you.)

Take Care Regarding Cancellation Your reception isn't likely to get canceled, but you never know. Find out the exact date by which you'd have to cancel your reservation to get your money back.

Do the Hotel Deal If your reception is in a hotel and many guests will be staying there, the hotel may charge you less since you're bringing in business. Negotiate; they should throw in perks, such as an upgrade to the honeymoon suite for you two.

Weather the Storm If your site is outdoors, have an alternative location in mind in case of a blizzard or heat wave.

Beware the Home Wedding It sounds like a great way to save, but renting everything that a hotel or banquet hall would supply can get costly. Also be sure to consider essentials such as parking, restrooms, and a foul-weather plan.

Ignore Know-It-Alls If you want to pass on being announced or doing the bouquet and garter toss, that's your choice—don't let a banquet manager tell you that you must do things a certain way. On the other hand, if the site manager has overseen lots of weddings, he or she is a valuable source of information about timing and other aspects of the party.

Take Your Time It's critical that your other vendors have the information and access they need to get their job done. Make sure your site manager will let them view the space in advance, as well as give them access as early as they need it on your wedding day.

Booking the Reception Site Checklist

☐ Visit favored sites during an event to investigate acoustics, true capacity, decorated look, and so forth.

    Location: _____ Date/time: _____

    Location: _____ Date/time: _____

☐ Ask favored sites to fax you a list of two or three wedding-couple references.

☐ Call references and the Better Business Bureau to check sites' record.

☐ Finalize your decision and reserve the site by phone. Send a fax to confirm.

☐ Request a contract and review for critical points:
  - Name and contact information for you and the vendor
  - Date and time frame of your reception (the average dinner-and-dance reception is about four hours long, longer if this includes the ceremony)
  - Exact names of specific room(s) to be used
  - What time other vendors (florist, DJ, and others) will be able to set up
  - Approximate number of guests and number of tables to be set up (include a floor plan if possible)
  - The name of the manager on duty during your reception
  - Itemized list of what the site will provide (from wait staff to linens, plus services such as coatroom and valet parking)
  - Proof of insurance and liquor license
  - Setup, cleanup, overtime, and any other fees
  - Total cost (itemized)
  - Deposit amount due
  - Balance and date due
  - Cancellation and refund policy
  - Site manager's signature

☐ Sign final contract.

☐ If your reception will be outdoors in a public place, file for a permit.

☐ Make a list of anything you'll need to rent (tent, tables, chairs, and so on) and look into rental companies; visit your site with your rental agent so he or she sees firsthand what you need (do all this about six to eight months before).

☐ Take pictures of the site to show to other wedding vendors.

☐ Ask for directions coming from various routes (you'll need this to include in invitations or post on your wedding Web page). Drive them yourself.

☐ Meet with or call the site manager to discuss decorations and final menu decisions if you're working with in-house people, or to coordinate plans with outside caterers, florists, and other vendors (do this at least four months before).

ALISON & CRAIG: AN OUTDOOR OCCASION

September 6
Annandale-On-Hudson, NY
Planning Time Frame: 18 Months

ALISON GREW UP spending summers in New York State's Catskill Mountains, so when she and Craig got engaged, they knew exactly where to look for a wedding site and they knew they wanted to celebrate outdoors. "We wanted to find something breathtaking, where people could get a real sense of the countryside," Alison says. "Something very natural, but elegant at the same time." The couple explored the Hudson Valley and settled on Montgomery Place, an historic estate located on a bluff overlooking the Hudson River. Nearby was the charming town of Rhinebeck, full of quaint inns perfect for out-of-town guests and the wedding party.

Next, the couple hired a local caterer. "In many ways she acted as a wedding planner. She made the arrangements for renting a tent, tables, chairs, and linens," Alison says. After a traditional Jewish ceremony with the river as a backdrop, guests enjoyed hors d'oeuvres on the lawn and then made their way to the tent for dinner. "We planned the food around the fact that it was outdoors," Alison says. "We wanted everything to be mesquite grilled, so you could smell the food grilling." Lamb, as well as grilled potatoes and vegetables, were featured. As favors, guests received sparklers to light when the sun went down. "That's something you couldn't do at an indoor wedding," Alison points out. "We ended up with the most amazing pictures—the hills, my veil wafting in the breeze."

Alison and Craig's Outdoor Wedding Tips

- Have a backup plan. If it looked like rain, Alison and Craig's caterer was going to order an additional tent for the ceremony.
- Prepare your guests. "In my family, a standard wedding is at a banquet hall in the city," says Alison. "I wanted people to know that this might not be typical." She sent letters suggesting that female guests bring wraps in case the temperature dropped after sundown, and golf carts were available to transport older guests to the restrooms and from the site's parking lot to the wedding area.
- Don't be a control freak. "I wouldn't advise an outdoor wedding if you're someone who needs everything to be perfect. There was always the lingering chance that the weather could interfere."
- You won't have to splurge on flowers. An outdoor site can trim your florist bill—the setting is already bucolic and beautiful.

CONTACT CHEAT SHEET:
Reception Site

Name: _____

Address: _____

_____

Contact: _____

Phone: _____

Fax: _____

E-mail: _____

Web site: _____

Room(s) and time reserved: _____

_____

Estimate: $_____

Deposit: $_____   Date paid: ____ / ____ / ____

Total cost: $_____

Balance: $_____   Date due: ____ / ____ / ____

staple business card here

Notes

_____
_____
_____
_____
_____
_____
_____
_____
_____
_____
_____
_____
_____
_____

CONTACT CHEAT SHEET:
Rental Company

Name: _____

Address: _____

Contact: _____

Phone: _____

Fax: _____

E-mail: _____

Items to be rented:

- ☐ Tent
- ☐ Chairs # _____
- ☐ Cake table
- ☐ Dinnerware

    Place settings # _____   Hors d'oeuvres plates # _____

    Dessert plates # _____   Serving pieces # _____

    Flatware sets # _____   Extra forks, or other # _____

- ☐ Glassware

    Champagne flutes # _____   Water glasses # _____

    White wine # _____   Bar glasses # _____

    Red wine # _____   _____ # _____

- ☐ Linens

    Tablecloths # _____   Napkins # _____

    Chair covers # _____   Overlays or skirting # _____

    - ☐ Other (dance floor, candelabras, portable toilets, or other)

- ☐ Bar/serving tables # _____
- ☐ Dining tables # _____ (to seat # _____ each)
- ☐ Head tables # _____

_____   _____

_____   _____

_____   _____

Estimate: $_____

Deposit: $_____   Date paid: ____ / ____ / ____

Total cost: $_____

Balance: $_____   Date due: ____ / ____ / ____

the dress

Not to make you nervous, but you are about to buy the most expensive, stared-at, must-be-perfect piece of clothing you'll ever wear. Your dress is the wedding's true centerpiece. Remember these three things: (1) Start shopping as soon as possible, as in nine to twelve months (or more) before the wedding—it will take the pressure off the process. Place your order according to the time suggested by the manufacturer. (2) You'll have found it when you look in the mirror and feel absolutely fabulous. (3) Consider your accessories carefully—they need to complement your overall look.

The Bride's Look Worksheet

Before you get lost in all of your dress options, try to get an idea of what you imagine yourself wearing. As you begin to get out there and look (the ten-thousand-plus-image wedding gown guide on TheKnot.com is the best place to begin), try to identify the features you like most.

Style (check all that apply)

☐ Formal   ☐ Informal   ☐ Traditional
☐ Unusual   ☐ Classic   ☐ Modern
☐ Cinderella-esque   ☐ Romantic   ☐ Spare & simple
☐ Ornate   ☐ Lots of coverage   ☐ Supersexy

Shape

☐ Ball gown   ☐ Sheath   ☐ A-line (princess)

Features

Neckline
☐ Jewel-neck
☐ Sweetheart
☐ Sabrina
☐ Off-the-shoulder
☐ Scoop neck
☐ Halter

Length
☐ Floor-length
☐ Knee-length
☐ More train
☐ Less train
☐ Detachable train

Adornment
☐ Sleeveless
☐ Short or cap sleeves
☐ Long sleeves
☐ Beading, lace
☐ Unadorned

Color

☐ White-white   ☐ Off-white, ivory, cream, candlelight
☐ Champagne   ☐ Rum pink
☐ Other color _____

Accessories (choose any that apply)

On head
☐ Long veil
☐ Minimal veil
☐ Tiara
☐ Barrettes

On arms
☐ Long gloves
☐ Short gloves
☐ Wrap or shawl
☐ Cape or coat

On feet
☐ Strappy sandals
☐ Bare feet
☐ Pumps
☐ Slingbacks or mules

Jewelry

_____

_____

Wedding dress and accessories budget $_____

Calling All Bridal Salons

Research stores by asking newlywed friends, looking at ads in national and/or local wedding magazines to see which stores sell dresses you like, and asking other wedding professionals for referrals. You can browse thousands of gowns and catalogs from over 150 designers at **www.TheKnot.com/bridalsearch**.

Make appointments at several bridal salons:

Name: _____   Name: _____

Address: _____   Address: _____

_____   _____

Contact: _____   Contact: _____

Phone: _____   Phone: _____

Web site: _____   Web site: _____

Referred by: _____   Referred by: _____

App't date: ___ /___/ ___ Time: _____   App't date: ___ /___/ ___ Time: _____

Notes: _____   Notes: _____

_____   _____

_____   _____

_____   _____

Favorite designers & styles: _____

_____

_____

_____

_____

_____

_____

Questions to Ask Bridal Salons

☐ What size sample dresses are available to try on? (Most stores only have samples in a size 8 or 10.)

☐ Can you look through the dresses yourself, or does the salesperson bring them out? (Many stores will let you look through samples to get an idea of what you like; then the salesperson brings you gowns to try on based on your preferences.)

☐ Does the store carry the designers you are interested in?

☐ _____   ☐ _____

☐ _____   ☐ _____

☐ _____   ☐ _____

☐ Does the store carry dresses in your price range? $ _____

☐ Does the store have shoes and undergarments to try on with gowns, or must you bring your own? (Find out when you call to make your appointment.)

☐ If you like a dress that the store doesn't carry, will it order a sample for you to try on? (Just keep in mind that you may then be obligated to buy the dress. Find out if the store is able to borrow a sample from the manufacturer.)

☐ How long does it generally take for a dress to come in after it's been ordered? (It usually takes three to four months.) Can the order be rushed, if necessary?

☐ Can you see a fabric sample for the dress you're interested in ordering? (Sample dresses you try on may be worn from wear, and the shade may not be true.)

☐ Does the store carry headpieces and other accessories (purses, gloves, shoes)? If not, can they suggest other places to shop?

☐ Can you get a written alteration estimate when you order your dress? (It's difficult to tell exactly what needs to be altered until the dress comes in, but ask for a basic price list. This should be a flat fee or even included.)

☐ If your bridesmaids order their dresses through this store, do you receive a discount?

☐ Ask for recommendations based on:

  ☐ What style, shape, color, and details you're thinking of:_____

  _____

  ☐ The formality of your wedding: _____

Knot Knowledge: Dress Shopping Tips & Tricks

What It Costs Dress prices range widely—from $750 to $15,000. The average gown is around $2,000. Dresses in the lower price ranges are typically made in assembly-line fashion; couture dresses are more personally handcrafted. Don't forget to factor in the cost of your veil and headpiece (they can cost between $100 and $350) as well as accessories such as shoes, lingerie, jewelry, and a purse, all of which can run from $50 to $350 each.

Ways to Save Avoid ornate, hand-done beading or lacework. Shop sample sales for floor models at discounts. Wear Mom's dress. Consider a bridesmaid's dress in white. Choose a simple headpiece and shoes. Try a consignment shop. Rent.

Size It Up Forget about your regular dress size. Bridal sizes run small, and each wedding dress manufacturer actually has its own sizing chart. A knowledgeable store will know how that designer's dresses are supposed to fit. Know, too, that every dress needs alterations. When it is altered correctly, you should be able to move comfortably and the dress should stay in place.

Research Your Religion Many churches and synagogues consider bare shoulders disrespectful. Ask your officiant, and get yourself a wrap or bolero jacket if you simply must have a spaghetti-strap or strapless gown.

Be Sure Don't buy the first dress you try on, even if you love it. Give yourself all the options and the time to think. Because gowns are custom-made, once you've ordered, there's no turning back. Expect strict (or nonexistent) cancellation and refund policies.

Shop an Authorized Store If you buy a gown from a shop not authorized to sell that designer's line, there's no guarantee that your dress is going to arrive on time, if at all. If you're unsure whether a shop is authorized, call the manufacturer. (Up-to-date manufacturer phone numbers are online at TheKnot.com.)

Know What You're Getting Many stores tear the labels out of sample dresses, citing the risk of price competition. But if you are ready to buy a dress, you have a right to know who the designer is. Get a name or go elsewhere.

Shop During Off Hours Take time off during the week, day or evening, to shop— you'll get more of the salespeople's time and attention. At most salons you'll need an appointment.

Keep an Open Mind The most elegant gowns often have the least presence or appeal on the hanger. Try various silhouettes; you never know what's going to flatter you best until you do.

Don't Travel With an Entourage One to three fellow shoppers is sufficient. Too many opinions will just overwhelm you.

Size Matters If you are a voluptuous bride, find a salon that carries samples in a size to suit you (many do these days). There are also designers who specialize in styles for larger sizes. Log onto **www.TheKnot.com/plussize** for listings.

Try a Trunk Show If you find a designer you like, visit during these in-store events featuring a specific designer (or a representative of a manufacturer) and his or her entire line. You'll get an opportunity to see and/or purchase every dress in the line, not just the styles that store chose to sell that season. And you may also get to chat with the designer

Accessorize with Care If your dress is ornate, stick with plain shoes, an unadorned veil, and a basic purse. The opposite also applies—a simple dress can stand an embellished veil or fun hat, a feathered or beaded purse, and strappy sandals.

Wedding Gown Checklist

☐ Choose your gown. If possible, also select your headpiece now.

☐ Get measured (bust, waist, and hips—and possibly shoulders, based on the dress style).

☐ Decide what size to order. Ask to see the manufacturer's sizing chart yourself; choose the size that fits your largest measurement.

☐ Request a letter of agreement or review your receipt for the following critical points:
  - Name and contact information for you and the salon
  - Your wedding date
  - A detailed description of your dress, including:
    Designer or manufacturer name
    Style number
    Color
    Fabric
    Size ordered
  - Any special requests (extra length, beading, different sleeves, and so on)
  - Date the dress will be delivered to the store
  - Descriptions of any accessories you order
  - Total price, itemized for the dress, headpiece, alteration estimate, and any other accessories or services (such as steaming)
  - Deposit amount due
  - Balance and date due
  - Cancellation and refund policy
  - Salesperson's/owner's signature

☐ Keep a copy of receipt.

Attire Etiquette

Q: Which dress silhouettes flatter which figures?

A: You should definitely try on several different silhouettes to find the one that looks best on you, but here are some general guidelines:

- Petite: Consider a columnlike sheath or a high-waisted dress to add length. Look for something simple with detail around the shoulders, to bring the focus up to your face. An open neck is also flattering to a petite woman. Avoid a wide border around the skirt hem.
- Full-figured and curvy: Try dresses with a Basque waist—a natural waist with a V front and full skirt, which has a slimming effect on the waist and hips. A high-waisted dress with a low neckline also flatters curves.
- Thick/undefined waist: Try on an empire-waist dress—a small bodice and slender skirt that falls in a slight A line from right below the bustline. If you have a large chest or hips, you probably want to stay away from this one.
- Short-waisted (or any shape): Try princess, or A-line, dresses, with seams running from the shoulders to the hem but with no seams on the waist, for a long, slim look. This style works on just about every figure.
- Boyish figure: A traditional ball gown may be for you, fitted through the bodice to the waist with a full skirt. It's a very feminine shape that adds curves.

Q: This is my second wedding. Can I wear white?

A: Yes, of course! White simply represents joy and celebration and is just as much your terrain as that of the first-time bride. If you don't feel comfortable in an elaborate ball gown, go for a simpler dress with a modest headpiece. Whether to wear a veil is up to you.

Q: I'm wearing elbow-length gloves with my dress. What do I do with them during the ring ceremony, and are there any rules for when I should take them off later in the day?

A: A no-fuss solution: Make a slit in the seam of the ring finger on your left glove, so you can slip your finger out to receive your wedding ring. You should definitely take gloves off when you're in the receiving line—shaking hands is something to do bare! Also remove them anytime you eat or drink during the day. This may become a pain, and you might just decide to take them off for good once you get to the reception.

Q: What's the etiquette of veils? Who lifts my veil during the ceremony, and when? Do I wear it throughout my reception?

A: How much veiling to wear for your ceremony is up to you—some brides opt for a hat, headband, or fresh flowers instead; others go for yards of fabric and a "blusher" veil to hide their face. Depending on your ceremony (and possibly religious requirements), your father can lift up a face veil when the two of you reach the altar or stage and he gives you a kiss, or you might wear it draped over your face until the exchange of vows and the kiss, when the groom does the honors. Many brides choose to wear their veil during the reception (minus the blusher, of course), but others find it unwieldy. You might want to consider a veil attached to the headpiece with Velcro, which can be easily removed without disturbing your hairdo for the party.

Fittings & Accessories Checklist

☐ Based on when your dress is expected to come in (probably within three to six months), schedule a first fitting. Date: _____ / _____ / _____ Time:_____

☐ About a month after you order, call the shop to confirm your delivery date.

☐ Make a list of all accessories you'll need, and start to purchase them (you'll want lingerie and shoes in time for your first fitting):

    ☐ Bustier/bra
    ☐ Garter
    ☐ Slip
    ☐ Stockings
    ☐ Petticoat
    ☐ Crinoline
    ☐ Pumps
    ☐ Sandals
    ☐ Wrap
    ☐ Purse
    ☐ Gloves
    ☐ Jewelry

☐ Search for accessories at **www.TheKnot.com/accessories**.

☐ When the dress comes in, go try it on and check it over carefully. Make sure it's the style you ordered and that nothing is damaged.

☐ Have your first fitting. (The salesperson or seamstress will pin the dress in places you need it taken in.)

☐ Schedule a second fitting (when you'll try on the altered dress to make sure it fits). Date: _____ / _____ / _____ Time:_____

☐ If you haven't yet, decide on a headpiece.

☐ At your second fitting, determine whether your dress fits you properly. (If it does, the store will press it for you and you can take it home.)

☐ If more alterations are necessary, schedule a third fitting. (Two are usually sufficient.) Date: _____ / _____ / _____ Time:_____

CONTACT CHEAT SHEET: Bridal Salon

Salon: _____

Address: _____

_____

Contact: _____

Phone: _____

Fax: _____

Store hours: _____

Dress designer: _____

Style number: _____

Price: $ _____

Alteration estimate: $ _____

Accessories (list, with prices): _____

_____

_____

Total cost $ _____

Deposit $ _____   Date paid: _____ / _____ / _____

Balance $ _____   Date due: _____ / _____ / _____

Date dress will be in: _____

Dates of fittings:

    First   _____ / _____ / _____

    Second   _____ / _____ / _____

    Third   _____ / _____ / _____

staple business card here

Notes

_____

_____

_____

_____

_____

_____

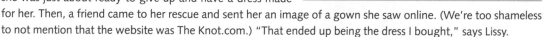

LISSY & JOSH: THE SEARCH FOR THE PERFECT GOWN

November 16
Houston, Texas
Planning Time: Seven Months

LISSY THOUGHT finding her dream dress was impossible. She had a very specific, very "Grace Kelly" aesthetic in mind. "I loved her wedding gown, with the high lace neck and long sleeves," says Lissy. With only two weeks to find "the one" (she travels a lot and her very particular planning schedule allowed for only fourteen days to find her gown), she was just about ready to give up and have a dress made for her. Then, a friend came to her rescue and sent her an image of a gown she saw online. (We're too shameless to not mention that the website was The Knot.com.) "That ended up being the dress I bought," says Lissy.

The gown, designed by Carolina Herrera, was an A-line, floor-length, double-faced white duchesse satin with a high round collar, capped sleeves, and a belt at the natural waist which tied to a bow in the back. An added retro touch: a keyhole opening in the back of her gown.

Though she was satisfied, the shopping experience wasn't over yet. Since she and her fiancé, Josh, had hired KC and the Sunshine Band to perform at their reception, Lissy knew most of the day she'd be dancing and didn't want to be shimmying across the dance floor in a constricting, and somewhat hot, dress. So, a seamstress at Carolina Herrera in New York City made her a "cooler" version of her gown for the reception. After the ceremony, Lissy changed into the knee-length skirt and a sleeveless top with a high collar that allowed her plenty of movement to kick her heels off and "do a little dance."

Lissy's Dress Shopping Tips

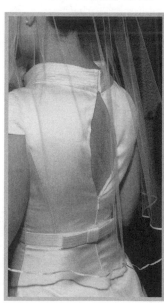

- RESEARCH. Despite Lissy's lack of time to do much research, she suggests looking in magazines, in books, and online to find styles that suit you. "You can even look at movies for inspiration," says Lissy, who found her muse in the 1950s star.
- RESPECT. A good relationship with your gown designer and seamstress is everything. Says Lissy, "Make sure that you respect the person helping you with your gown and that they respect you. Be on time for your appointments and fittings. In return, make sure they don't shuttle you off quickly to get to the newest customer coming into the store."
- REBEL. Shop solo! Gasp, gasp. "I know all the best friends, mothers, and aunts out there will kill me for saying this, but go shopping alone," says Lissy. "At least at first." Everyone will have her own opinion of which gown you should buy, but it's harder to know which one you favor when you're feeling pressure or influence. In the end, the choice is yours.

CONTACT CHEAT SHEET:
Hair & Makeup

Hairstylist: _____

Address: _____

_____

Contact: _____

Phone: _____

Fax: _____

Store hours: _____

Date/time of appointment(s): _____ /_____ /_____

_____

Total cost (plus tip): $_____

staple business card here

Makeup artist: _____

Address: _____

_____

Contact: _____

Phone: _____

Fax: _____

Store hours: _____

Date/time of appointment(s): _____ /_____ /_____

_____

Total cost (plus tip): $_____

staple business card here

Notes

_____

_____

_____

_____

_____

_____

_____

Notes

food & drink

Your wedding feast will by far be your largest expense. It's also one of the things your event will most be remembered by. Start making decisions in this arena early. Your caterer and reception site go hand in hand: If you're using an on-site caterer, carefully interview them before you book the reception site. If your caterer is independent, decide what to serve (brunch, tea, dinner) soon so that you can determine the appropriate time to reserve the site.

Wedding Food Worksheet

Before you lock in a caterer, check the box(es) under each heading that best describe your image of your wedding meal. If you have no idea, then leave it to discuss in your meetings with caterers.

Meal
- ☐ Brunch
- ☐ Lunch
- ☐ Tea
- ☐ Cocktails
- ☐ Dinner
- ☐ Dessert only

Service
- ☐ Cocktails (☐ Passed hors d'oeuvres ☐ Hors d'oeuvres tables)
- ☐ Seated meal
  - ☐ Family-style
  - ☐ American
  - ☐ French
  - ☐ Russian (white-gloved)
- ☐ Buffet
  - ☐ Formal (staff-served)
  - ☐ Casual (self-serve)
  - ☐ Food stations (for example, raw bar, crepe table)

Flavor
- ☐ Continental
- ☐ Regional
- ☐ Seasonal
- ☐ Ethnic _____
- ☐ Thematic _____

Courses
- ☐ Hors d'oeuvres
- ☐ Appetizer
- ☐ Salad
- ☐ Soup
- ☐ Fruit and cheese
- ☐ Pasta
- ☐ Dessert

Requirements
- ☐ Kosher
- ☐ Vegetarian
- ☐ Other _____

Entrées
- ☐ Beef
- ☐ Chicken
- ☐ Vegetarian
- ☐ Pork
- ☐ Seafood
- ☐ Lamb
- ☐ Pasta

Other food ideas _____
_____
_____
_____

Dessert
- ☐ Cake only
- ☐ Additional desserts

Alcohol
- ☐ Full bar (☐ Open ☐ Limited)
- ☐ Beer and wine only
- ☐ Wine with dinner
- ☐ Champagne toast
- ☐ Specialty cocktail

Catering Budget
Total: $ _____ ÷ # of guests _____ = $ _____ per head

Calling All Caterers

Hotels, country clubs, and other large special-event facilities will likely have in-house caterers or preferred-caterer lists. Favorite restaurants may cater; also, log onto **www.TheKnot.com/caterers** to find a list of good ones in your area. Check ads in regional and/or national bridal or city magazines. You can call the National Association of Catering Executives at 847-480-9080 for a local referral.

Make appointments with several caterers:

Company: _____   Company: _____

Contact: _____   Contact: _____

Address: _____   Address: _____

Phone: _____   Phone: _____

Referred by: _____   Referred by: _____

App't date: ___/___/___ Time: _____   App't date: ___/___/___ Time: _____

Price range: $ _____ – _____ per head   Price range: $ _____ – _____ per head

Notes: _____   Notes: _____

_____   _____

_____   _____

_____   _____

_____   _____

_____   _____

Do-It-Yourself Drink Decoder

Purchasing the alcohol yourselves is a good money-saving option. Use this worksheet to figure out amounts and double-check your math with your caterer or bartender. These are averages. You know your crowd best, so buy accordingly (that is, if your friends love to do tequila shots, one bottle won't be enough).

☐ Determine how much of each alcohol you need for each aspect of your reception:

Open-bar amounts (per 100 people):

Fluid	# per 100 guests	Your Totals
Champagne	18 bottles	_____
Red wine	10 bottles	_____
White wine	18 bottles	_____
Beer	2–3 cases	_____
Whiskey	1–2 liters	_____
Bourbon	1–2 liters	_____
Gin	2 liters	_____
Scotch	3 liters	_____
Rum	2 liters	_____
Vodka	6 liters	_____
Tequila	1 liter	_____
Dry vermouth	2 bottles	_____
Sweet vermouth	2 bottles	_____
Tonic	1 case	_____
Club soda	1 case	_____
Cranberry juice	2 gallons	_____
Orange juice	1 gallon	_____
Grapefruit juice	1 gallon	_____
Other (for specialty cocktail): _____		_____
_____		_____

Champagne toast: 1½ cases (18 bottles) per 100 guests _____
(assumes 6 glasses per bottle, 1 glass per person)

Wine for dinner: 4+ cases (50 bottles) per 100 guests _____
(assumes 4–6 glasses per bottle, 2 glasses per person)

Note: If you are serving white, buy more; if you are serving red, buy shy (in other words, people tend to drink more when they drink white wine). If you are serving both red and white, the breakdown should be about fifty-fifty, or two cases red and two cases white per hundred people.

☐ Locate a liquor discounter or wholesaler. (If your caterer cannot provide you with a referral, look in the yellow pages under "Liquor" for ads that mention discounts and delivery.)

Company: _____   Company: _____

Contact: _____   Contact: _____

Address: _____   Address: _____

Phone: _____   Phone: _____

Fax: _____   Fax: _____

Price quote: $ _____   Price quote: $ _____

Notes: _____   Notes: _____

_____   _____

_____   _____

☐ Send list of needs to two liquor suppliers and ask for detailed price quote (including tax and delivery charge, if any).
☐ Find out when you need to deliver liquor to caterer.
☐ Order and pay for with credit card.
☐ Make sure you are faxed a written receipt that includes:
    ☐ List of all items and amounts ordered
    ☐ What items (if any) will arrived chilled
    ☐ Delivery date, time
    ☐ Exact delivery address
☐ Confirm that caterer or bartender is supplying tools (shakers, ice tongs, etc.)
☐ Confirm that caterer or bartender will do all prep work (for example, cutting limes)
☐ Confirm that caterer is renting enough glasses for the drinking you have envisioned (for example, if you are having a champagne toast, you will need a flute for each guest).
☐ When alcohol is delivered, expect to tip at least $20–$30.

Knot Knowledge: Food & Drink Tips

What it Costs Prices are usually quoted per head. A dinner can range in cost from $40 to $300 a guest. Make sure you know exactly what is included in any estimate: taxes, gratuities, rentals, and so on. If gratuities will be included in your final bill, ask whether they are calculated before or after taxes.

Ways to Save Serve tea or cocktails instead of dinner. Cut down on dinner courses. Keep your menu simple. Avoid expensive ingredients (wild mushrooms, salmon steaks, and so on). Opt for pasta and chicken as entrées. Savor specialties of the season and region. Buy your own alcohol. Limit your bar.

Try Ethnic Eats Wedding food doesn't have to be boring. Find a caterer that serves (or is inspired by) festive cuisines such as Italian, Caribbean, Mexican, soul, Cajun, or Greek. It may be more economical, and it will certainly be more interesting. Just beware if there are picky eaters among your guests.

Tasting Tips Don't choose your caterer based solely on your tasting. (It's easy to cook a good meal for two people. Checking references will let you know whether a caterer's skills extend to large groups.) Also, try at least two items for each course so you'll have an alternative if your original idea doesn't pan out.

Be Careful with Restaurants Serving a group of two hundred and preparing plates one by one are two different things. If you choose restaurant catering, make sure the place has wedding experience, the appropriate equipment, and service-oriented staff.

Make a Printed Menu If you're serving intriguing foods or using ingredients with special significance, explain them on a printed menu placed on each table. Make sure it matches your caterer's final list.

Focus on Service Good food is only half the battle. Ask references whether the staff went the distance to ensure guests were served in an appropriately beautiful, friendly, fast, and attentive manner.

Curb Corkage Fees Purchase a set amount of liquor yourselves if you can; if bartenders simply open new bottles as needed, the cost per bottle opened (the corkage fee) can get astronomical. Also, have someone watch over the bottle counting; it is easy to make a mistake.

Beware the Beer and Wine Option People often limit drink options to beer and wine to help contain costs, but keep in mind that wine may well be pricier than hard alcohol—you'll get about five drinks out of a bottle of wine and twenty out of a bottle of alcohol.

Serve a Specialty Cocktail A great way to add color and festive flair is to offer a special drink in addition to (or in lieu of) champagne. Consider something thematic: spiked eggnog or cider during winter; rum punch or piña coladas for island flavor; cosmopolitans or martinis for an urban-lounge-like feel.

Questions to Ask Caterers

☐ Does the caterer specialize in certain types of food or service? (They should provide you with sample menus to look at.)

☐ Will the caterer arrange for a tasting of the foods you might be interested in serving prior to your hiring them? (They should.)

☐ What is the caterer's average price range? Are costs itemized depending on the foods you choose, or is there an all-inclusive flat rate? What would that include? Does the caterer have printed price sheets for food selections?

☐ How involved is the caterer in a typical reception—does he or she work like a wedding coordinator or banquet manager, cueing the band, telling the couple when to cut the cake, adjusting the schedule if guests aren't ready to sit down to dinner? (You will need to find someone to fill this role—if your site manager or caterer isn't going to do this, you may want to hire a coordinator for the day.)

☐ Who would be your main contact? Will the same person you work with when planning also oversee meal service on your wedding day? (You want this to be the case if at all possible.)

☐ Is the caterer working any other weddings on the same weekend, on the same day, or at the same time as yours?

☐ If your reception site can't, can the caterer provide tables, chairs, linens, and dinnerware? (Ask to see linens, serving pieces, and the like to make sure they're acceptable to you.) Will they arrange for the rentals, if required? (Try to avoid handling the rentals yourself.)

☐ Does the caterer set the tables? And put out place cards and favors?

☐ Will the caterer provide wait staff? How many would they recommend for the size of your wedding? What do wait staff wear? (Top caterers say they always use their own serving personnel, even if the site's staff is available, because they understand the caterer's expectations and way of doing business.)

☐ Where will food be prepared? Are there on-site facilities, or do you, the caterer, and the site need to make additional arrangements? (If the caterer has to bring in his or her own equipment, is there an additional fee?)

☐ Does the caterer work with fresh (not frozen) food?

☐ Does the caterer have a license? (This means the business has met health department standards and has liability insurance; make sure that includes a license to serve liquor if you're having a bar.)

☐ Can the caterer provide alcohol, or is/can the bar be your or the reception site's responsibility? (If you can provide it, is there a corkage fee? How and when do you get the alcohol to the caterer? If the caterer will provide it, do they have an inflexible wine list, or can you make special requests? How is it priced?)

☐ Can you see photographs of the caterer's previous work? (How the food is displayed is important. Fabulous food served in plastic buckets won't cut it.)

☐ Can you speak to previous wedding clients? (Get at least two references who had a similar number of guests and a similar style of menu.)

☐ Does the caterer also do wedding cakes? Can you use an outside baker if you desire? (Is there a cake-cutting fee? See page 160 for more information.)

Hiring the Caterer Checklist

☐ Arrange for tastings (if you didn't have one on your first visit).

Caterer: _____

Date: ____/____/____ Time: ____

Caterer: _____

Date: ____/____/____ Time: ____

☐ Ask each caterer to draw up a proposal, including:
- Cost per person
- Options for hors d'oeuvres, appetizer, entrées, and side dishes
- Exactly what the price includes: alcohol, rentals, gratuities, etc.
- Service and presentation style (how the food will be laid out)
- Less expensive alternatives
- References

☐ Call references and include the following questions:
- As background: number of guests, venue, menu
- Was the meal good, hot, and well presented?
- Were guests served and tables cleared efficiently?
- Any surprises on the final menu or final bill?

☐ Reserve your favorite caterer by phone. Send a fax to confirm wedding date.

☐ Finalize menu decisions:

Hors d'oeuvres _____

Appetizers _____

Salad or soup course _____

Entrée(s) _____

Side dishes _____

Cheese course _____

Drinks _____

Dessert _____

Cake _____

Other _____

☐ Finalize per person price: $ _____

☐ Request a contract.

☐ Review for critical points and revise as needed:
  - Name and contact information for you and the vendor
  - Date, starting time, and length of your reception
  - Location of reception, including the exact name of the room
  - Date the caterer needs a final head count
  - Staff: waiter-to-guest ratio, number of bartenders
  - Type of service (cocktails, buffet, tea, dessert, seated meal)
  - If buffet, how you will be charged (by guest or by plate count)
  - A specific menu (you may make alterations to this menu later)
  - Acceptable food substitutions (in case of unavailability on wedding day)
  - Liquor: what kinds, how much (if the caterer is handling it)
  - Cake: layers, flavor, ornamentation (if the caterer is handling it)
  - Rentals: what's included (tablecloths, napkins, dishes, tables, and so on)
  - The name of the person who will oversee your catering service
  - Proof of license and liability insurance
  - The approximate number of guests
  - Costs per person (three levels: adult, child, photographer or other vendor)
  - Detailed accounting of extra fees:
    - Sales tax
    - Fees for extra waiters
    - Delivery
    - Bar or corkage fee
    - Rentals
    - Gratuities
    - Kitchen fee
    - Cake-cutting fee
  - Overtime rates
  - Total estimated cost of the service
  - Deposit amount due
  - Balance and date due
  - Cancellation and refund policy
  - Caterer's signature

☐ Sign final contract.

☐ If any special facilities or equipment are needed at the reception site, schedule a meeting with the caterer and site manager to discuss and make arrangements.

Food & Drink Etiquette

Q: We don't have the budget to serve a full meal at our wedding reception. Is that okay? How do we make sure people don't expect one?

A: As long as you do not have lots of guests traveling from out of town, it's fine to skip the full meal. Some times of day dictate a meal, some don't. Here are the general guidelines for when people will be expecting meals: breakfast 9–11 A.M.; lunch, 11 A.M.–2 P.M.; brunch, 10 A.M.–3 P.M.; dinner, 6–9 P.M. To avoid serving a full meal, invite people for tea, 3–5 P.M.; cocktails, 5–7 P.M., or dessert, 9 P.M.–midnight. Just to be clear, add something along these lines to your invitation: "Please join us for cocktails [or tea, or champagne and cake, or light refreshments] immediately following the ceremony."

Q: We want to serve a buffet to save money. My parents think this is tacky. What would you do?

A: Here's my take on the buffet-vs.-seated-dinner debate: First off, be aware that a buffet isn't automatically cheaper than a seated meal. In fact, with all the heating equipment, extra food for presentation, and wait staff required to man one, it could actually be more expensive. (Same goes with passed vs. stationary hors d'oeuvres.) I've never minded buffets as a guest because your food stays hot, you get to mingle while you are in line, and you get to choose exactly what and how much you want. The best argument for the seated meal: You are literally waiting on your guests hand and foot. A good compromise is a family-style seated meal, where platters of food are brought by waiters and passed by the guests at the table.

Q: What's the best type of waiter service for a seated meal?

A: There are four service styles: American (plates prepared in the kitchen and brought out to guests by servers); family style (see above); French (waiters prepare food on tables or stands set up next to guest tables and serve individual plates); and Russian (white-gloved waiters actually carry each course on a large tray and serve each separately, directly to guests' plates). Your choice depends on the sense of formality you are trying to create. American is probably the most popular.

Q: Is it necessary to have seating arrangements, or should I just let guests sit wherever they want?

A: If you're serving a full meal, it makes sense to have seating arrangements. With cocktails, people like to mix and mingle, but when it comes to sitting down for dinner, they prefer knowing where they're supposed to go. Table cards are placed on an easily accessible table outside the main reception room, and they list each guest's (or couple's) name and the number or name of the table where they're sitting. Note: If you're doing a down-home country barbecue, and it's a really casual affair—and maybe there aren't too many guests, say fifty or less—it would be fine to let everyone sit wherever they want. (Just have more chairs than guests—you won't be able to get the guests to fill every seat at every table.)

Q: Is it okay to have a cash bar? We want our guests to be able to enjoy themselves, but we can't afford a lot of booze.

A: Don't make your guests pay for drinks at your wedding. If you can't afford a full open bar for the entire reception (lots of couples can't), consider limiting the hours the bar is open—maybe for two hours at the beginning of the reception, closed for an hour during the meal, then open for another hour afterward, but closing (still serving soft drinks) an hour before the reception ends (people have to drive home, remember). Buy liquor yourself from a wholesaler. Serve bar brands of hard liquor instead of brand names. In lieu of champagne, toast with whatever drink anyone has in hand.

CONTACT CHEAT SHEET: Caterer

Company: _____

Address: _____

_____

Contact: _____

Phone: _____

Fax: _____

staple business card here

Estimate $ _____ (per person)

Deposit $ _____   Date paid: ____/____/____

Total cost $ _____

Balance $ _____   Date due: ____/____/____

Notes

_____

_____

_____

_____

_____

_____

_____

_____

_____

_____

_____

_____

_____

_____

_____

_____

_____

_____

_____

Notes

gift registry

Why register for gifts? Because (1) it can be a lot of fun, (2) it makes your guests' lives easier, and (3) you'll actually get gifts you really want. Don't limit yourself to the traditional stuff; you can now register for everything from classy china to camping gear to cool cars. You'll want to make your wish list earlier than you'd think—about six to twelve months in advance—because you never know when you'll be thrown your engagement party or shower.

Wedding Gift Wish List Worksheet

Before you decide where you'll register, figure out what you really want. Try to find a registry that carries as many of your categories as possible to avoid guest confusion.

What you want (check all that apply)

- ☐ Cookware
- ☐ Fine and/or casual china
- ☐ Tools
- ☐ Food & wine
- ☐ Garden gear
- ☐ Linens
- ☐ Home or car down payment
- ☐ Camera/video equipment
- ☐ Music, books
- ☐ Other _____

- ☐ Home appliances
- ☐ Furniture
- ☐ Electronics
- ☐ Honeymoon travel
- ☐ Camping gear
- ☐ Computer equipment, software
- ☐ Stocks & bonds
- ☐ Lessons (dancing, cooking, etc.)
- ☐ Car, car payments

_____

_____

_____

_____

Registry features for you (check all that you'd like)

- ☐ Registry consultants
- ☐ Online registering
- ☐ Online list updating

- ☐ Batch delivery
- ☐ Incentives (contests, for example)
- ☐ Frequent-flyer mile programs

Registry features for your guests (check all that you'd like)

- ☐ Toll-free phone ordering
- ☐ Online ordering
- ☐ Local access by car

- ☐ National access via catalog
- ☐ National access via chain stores

Registering Online

It seemed so obvious. No sore feet, no traffic jams, no arguing in the aisles: Registering for gifts on the Internet was the ultimate invention. Enter: The Knot Wedding Gift Registry. The combination of ultra-convenience for guests, massive selection, and whip-smart customer service has made our online registry a no-brainer for thousands of brides and grooms. Check it out at: **www.TheKnot.com/registry**.

Calling All Registries

Research several registries online and off:

Registry: _____   Registry: _____

Address: _____   Address: _____

_____   _____

Phone:_____   Phone: _____

Web site: _____   Web site: _____

Contact: _____   Contact: _____

App't date: ___ /___/___ Time: _____   App't date: ___ /___/___ Time: _____

Notes: _____   Notes: _____

_____   _____

_____   _____

_____   _____

_____   _____

Questions to Ask Registry Consultants

☐ What range of products does the registry carry? What brands?

☐ Can gifts be shipped to an address you supply? (This is especially important if you're marrying in a town other than where you live.)

☐ Is your registry accessible online? Can guests purchase online? Can your registry list be faxed to faraway guests so they can order by phone?

☐ How does the store keep track of what's purchased? How often is it updated? (It should be updated instantly to protect you against getting duplicate gifts.)

☐ Will the person you're talking to be your store contact throughout the process? (Most places will assign you a registry consultant, someone who helps you make choices, keeps your list up to date, and so on.)

☐ What's the return policy? Can you bring back duplicate gifts or anything you decide you don't want for a store credit or exchange? Is there a time limit after the wedding to return things?

☐ Is there a completion program (you can fill in what guests didn't buy at a discount)? For how long after the wedding can you take advantage of it?

☐ How long after your wedding is your list kept active? (Should be at least a year.)

Knot Knowledge: Registering Tips

Expand Your Thinking You can now register for everything from bicycles to power tools to the down payment on a new home. Place settings are still very popular, but don't limit yourself to that. There's much else to consider.

Keep Prices in Mind Register for gifts in a range of prices so every guest will be able to afford something. Average amount spent: $50 to $150.

Consolidate It's hard to keep track of five different registries. Try to find a registry or store that has most of what you want all in one place.

Convenience Is King Make sure guests all over the country can access your registry online at any time, day or night.

Consider "Giftability" As much as you might need one, guests don't love giving bathmats as wedding gifts. Make sure you'd give what you want to get.

Update Your List Keep track of what gets bought. Add more items to your list once all that remains are the $10 kitchen gadgets and the $500 cookware set.

Gift Etiquette

Q: How do I get the word out about my registry? Can I put it on my invitation?

A: Make sure you tell your parents, attendants, and key friends where you are registered; it is their job to spread the word. You can give invitation inserts to your honor attendants to put in your shower invitations or to hand to anyone who asks. Don't ever print where you are registered on your invitation—some people are against that. Whether you include registry inserts in your invitations is up to you; mind you, some people are against it. One of the best ways to get the word out is to create a wedding Web page (you can do this easily at **www.TheKnot.com/pwp**) and link your registries from there. You e-mail guests with your Web page, and amid the rest of the information is a link to or listing of your registries.

Q: How do we let guests know we want cash instead of gifts?

A: Many guests *will* give you cash, without your having to ask—it's traditional in many parts of the country and among many ethnic groups, too (Chinese and Italian, to name but two). Otherwise, the best you can do is put your parents and wedding party on alert that if guests ask them what you'd most like for your wedding, they should say money. Then just cross your fingers! You should still register as a backup. Another strategy is to register for your honeymoon trip or for a down payment on a home. On TheKnot.com you can also register for gift certificates—for dinner at your favorite restaurant, car payments, classes—so guests will still feel they are getting you something specific, and you get what you really need.

Q: When do we need to start sending out thank-you notes for gifts, and do you have any advice?

A: Start sending out thank-you notes ASAP. It will feel like less of a chore if you do it as gifts come in, instead of waiting until you've got a hundred of them! Tips:
- *Time it right.* Try to send thank-yous for gifts received before the wedding within two weeks; after the wedding, within a month after the honeymoon. Do your best—and remember, it's *never* too late to send them.
- *Keep track.* Use the handy-dandy gift log on page 193 to record each guest's name, their gift, and the date you sent your note.
- *Do a few at a time.* Getting them all done in one sitting won't happen.
- *Divide and conquer.* The bride does her family and friends, the groom does his. Divide the mutual-friend pile evenly, or if one of you has a huge family and the other one's is pretty small, have the small-family person take care of friends.
- *Sign off.* Etiquette says that only the writer should sign, mentioning his or her spouse in the note ("Todd and I"), but lots of couples sign both their names.

Q: Are guests supposed to bring gifts to the wedding or ship them to the couple?

A: Most guests will know that the best thing to do is have gifts shipped to the address you give your registry (make sure they have the correct address—yours, your parents'—and ask that salespeople mention it when guests buy something). In some parts of the country, however, it is still traditional to bring gifts to the reception. To plan for it, arrange with the site manager for a safe place to put them—such as an attended coatroom, or a room or closet that can be locked. The best man and maid of honor are often responsible for collecting gift checks brought to the wedding.

Q: What do we do about damaged gifts?

A: If something arrives broken, check the box. If the gift's been sent from your registry, call their customer-service department to arrange for a replacement to be sent to you—there shouldn't be any charge.

Choosing & Managing the Registry Checklist

☐ Choose the store (or stores) at which you want to register.

☐ Have your registry consultant input your selections into the computer system and send you a list for verification.

☐ Check the list for accuracy of:
  ☐ Brand names
  ☐ Pattern names
  ☐ Colors
  ☐ Quantity

☐ Call the store with any changes (or better, make them before you leave).

☐ Let immediate family and wedding-party members know where you're registered, so they can tell shower guests and wedding guests who ask. If you prefer cash or decide not to register, let people know that, too.

☐ Ask the store for a registry list to be sure gifts are being deleted as they are purchased. Do this periodically (once a month, perhaps), starting as soon as gifts begin to arrive.

☐ Open gifts as you receive them and record who gives you what in the gift log on page 193. Keep packaging and cards with gifts to make it easier should you need to return anything.

CONTACT CHEAT SHEET: Registry

Registry: _____

Address: _____

_____

Consultant: _____

Phone: _____   Toll-free orders: _____

E-mail: _____

Fax: _____   Online orders: http:// _____

Registry: _____

Address: _____

_____

Consultant: _____

Phone: _____   Toll-free orders: _____

E-mail: _____

Fax: _____   Online orders: http:// _____

Registry: _____

Address: _____

_____

Consultant: _____

Phone: _____   Toll-free orders: _____

E-mail: _____

Fax: _____   Online orders: http:// _____

Notes

_____

_____

_____

_____

_____

YOONSUN & MICHAEL: REGISTERING ONLINE

September 5
Stockton, NJ

FOR YOONSUN AND MICHAEL, choosing where to register depended entirely on convenience. Owning their our own business and simultaneously renovating their apartment and planning a wedding left little time for browsing around department stores all day. "Registering online was a great relief to us because we could register at any time of day or night and we could be as indecisive as we wanted to," Yoonsun says with a laugh. "I could change my mind at three A.M.!" When she woke up with a panic attack, she could just log on and rearrange her list. "Registering online," said Yoonsun, "I could control when I 'shopped,' who I 'spoke' to, and, best of all, my feet didn't hurt and my head didn't ache."

Yoonsun and Michael found TheKnot.com product selection refreshing. "The department stores had a big selection, but most of it seemed too 'tea party'. We wanted the basics but cool, fun, different things, too." Michael—who had been completely uninterested in the entire registry process—suddenly found himself browsing and picked up a Sony PlayStation for the list. Yoonsun took advantage of the ability to create her own gift—$500 to put toward new furniture.

Yoonsun and Michael's guests found online the registry equally convenient. "They were thrilled about not having to run out to a store," says the bride. "Also, they told us that being able to actually see everything we chose, instead of reviewing a text-only list, was really helpful."

Yoonsun and Michael's Online Registry Tips

- Make sure your online registry has "registry consultants," real people there to answer your questions about products and procedures.
- Use your imagination. Think about all aspects of your lifestyle when you are registering. There's more to married life than steak knives and tea sets.
- Get the word out. Memorize the toll-free phone number—and make sure everyone knows they can purchase gifts over the phone! Carry a copy of your registry list with you at all times in case a friend or relative asks for one.

reception music

The right music can make (or break!) your reception. Whether you hire a band or a DJ, music sets the mood, so choose carefully. The first decision is band vs. DJ, and that will largely be determined by your budget. Once you've settled that, get started on your search; as always, the best professionals get booked unbelievably early.

Ceremony music

Style

- ☐ Live
- ☐ Recorded
- ☐ Vocal
- ☐ Instrumental
- ☐ Soloist
- ☐ Ensemble
- ☐ Ethnic
- ☐ Folksy
- ☐ Classical
- ☐ Religious

Specific ideas: _____

_____

Hours needed: _____

Ceremony music budget: $ _____

Cocktail hour music

Style

- ☐ Live
- ☐ Recorded
- ☐ Laid-back
- ☐ Soloist
- ☐ Ensemble
- ☐ High-energy
- ☐ Vocal
- ☐ Instrumental
- ☐ Ethnic
- ☐ Folksy
- ☐ Classical
- ☐ Lounge-y

Specific ideas: _____

_____

Hours needed: _____

Cocktail hour budget: $ _____

Reception music

Talent

- ☐ Band
- ☐ DJ
- ☐ Large combo
- ☐ Small ensemble
- ☐ Vocals
- ☐ Instrumental

Genre

- ☐ Rock/pop
- ☐ Funk/hip-hop
- ☐ Latin
- ☐ R&B
- ☐ Country
- ☐ Dance mixes
- ☐ Big band/swing
- ☐ Reggae

Favorite songs: _____

_____

Ethnic dances: _____

_____

Hours needed: _____

Reception music budget: $ _____

Calling All Ceremony & Cocktail Hour Musicians

Make appointments with several musicians, vocalists, or groups:

Name: _____

Phone: _____

Referred by: _____

App't date: ___ /___/___ Time: _____

Type of music: _____

Price estimate: $_____/hr

Notes: _____

_____

_____

Name: _____

Phone: _____

Referred by: _____

App't date: ___ /___/___ Time: _____

Type of music: _____

Price estimate: $_____/hr

Notes: _____

_____

_____

Name: _____

Phone: _____

Referred by: _____

App't date: ___ /___/___ Time: _____

Type of music: _____

Price estimate: $_____/hr

Notes: _____

_____

_____

Name: _____

Phone: _____

Referred by: _____

App't date: ___ /___/___ Time: _____

Type of music: _____

Price estimate: $_____/hr

Notes: _____

_____

_____

Questions to Ask Ceremony & Cocktail Hour Musicians

☐ Has the musician (or group) played many weddings?

☐ Can you hear him or her play or sing, either privately or at a public performance (if you haven't already)? Request a tape.

☐ Is the musician familiar with the music you want? Must you supply sheet music?

☐ Will the musician bring his or her own equipment (music stands, microphones, and so on), or do you or the site need to supply it?

☐ How much room will the musician need?

☐ If you're hiring a vocalist or additional musicians to be accompanied by the church organist or other in-house musicians, will everyone be available to rehearse before your wedding and at the ceremony rehearsal?

☐ What will the musician wear?

☐ How much setup time is needed?

☐ What is the musician's fee for a wedding ceremony (probably about two hours of work)? Must you pay travel expenses as well?

ASK CARLEY
Reception Music Etiquette & Issues

Q: How do we choose between a band and a DJ?

A: Beyond budget, there are three factors: (1) authenticity—with a DJ, the songs you hear will be the original versions you're familiar with, whereas a band will play their own interpretations; (2) the action factor—live entertainment has a different feel than recorded music; and (3) space considerations.

Q: What do we do for music during the cocktail hour?

A: Cocktail hours need their own ambiance and are often a good place to be more unique or eclectic musically. Interesting options are a klezmer, steel-drum, bluegrass, or mariachi band. Also consider asking whether a few of the reception-band members are available to be your jazz combo or torch-song quartet during cocktails. You'll just tack the extra fee onto what you're already paying, as opposed to contracting with a whole new group. Do make sure they are going to sound different, not just like a smaller version of the band your guests will hear later.

Q: Do we have to play those silly wedding songs like the Hokey Pokey, Chicken Dance, and Electric Slide at our wedding?

A: Of course not, and if you don't want them, be clear with your entertainment about it. But if you dig deep down into your subconscious, we'll bet you actually like at least one of those wacky dances! The bottom line is that these group events are fun and familiar. It's completely up to you whether to omit or keep them, but consider your guests' preferences when you decide. And keep in mind that they're a great way to get people out on the dance floor.

Calling All Reception Bands & DJs

To find reception bands or DJs, get referrals from local or national musicians' unions or DJ associations; go to **www.TheKnot.com/local** to find one in your region; check local wedding or music magazines; see local gigs in clubs or other people's weddings or other special occasions; call local radio stations (some radio DJs moonlight as wedding performers).

Make appointments with several bands or DJs:

Name: _____   Name: _____

Address: _____   Address: _____

_____   _____

Phone: _____   Phone: _____

Referred by: _____   Referred by: _____

App't date: ___ /___/___ Time: _____   App't date: ___ /___/___ Time: _____

Type of music: _____   Type of music: _____

Price estimate: $_____   Price estimate: $_____

Notes: _____   Notes: _____

_____   _____

_____   _____

_____   _____

_____   _____

_____   _____

_____   _____

Questions to Ask Reception Bands & DJs

☐ What's the band's signature sound? Are they a jazz band, rock band, "wedding band"? Find out what type of music they consider their forte.

☐ Does the DJ specialize in a certain type of music—Top 40, swing, jazz, country—or does he or she offer a variety of genres? Can you see a playlist?

☐ Is the band or DJ willing to mix it up a bit (play some standards in addition to their typical rock fare, for example)? Will they perform or play ethnic standards, such as the hora or tarantella, if requested?

☐ If there's a song you want played and the band isn't familiar with it, are they willing to learn it in time for your wedding? Will you need to supply the sheet music? If a DJ, can you lend your own CDs, or is he or she willing to buy what you'd like played?

☐ How do they feel about a request list? (Answer should be along the lines of "We'll try to honor your requests, but we also need to measure the crowd.")

☐ How many band members are available? If you're interviewing a DJ, does he or she work with a partner, assistant, or dancers?

☐ Does the band or DJ bring equipment (amps, mikes, and so on), or would you and/or your reception site need to supply it?

☐ How much room will the band or DJ need? Will a DJ need a table to set up on?

☐ How much time before the reception would the band or DJ need to set up?

☐ Is there a minimum amount of time the band or DJ will play?

☐ How many breaks does the band or DJ typically take? Will they break in rotation, so someone is always playing? Or will they play taped music during breaks?

☐ What will the band or DJ wear?

☐ How much does the band or DJ charge for a four- or five-hour reception? If there is a range, what accounts for the difference between the high and low prices?

☐ What is the overtime policy? Is the charge per hour or half hour?

☐ Ask yourself: Does the band or DJ seem flexible and willing to play the music you want? (You'll want to give them some freedom, but if you sense that they are resistant to your desires, reconsider.)

Knot Knowledge: Reception Music Tips & Trends

What It Costs For a four-piece ensemble, you'll typically pay $1,000 to $4,000 for a four- or five-hour reception. Most DJs charge from $500 to $2,000 for that same amount of time. If you live in a large metropolitan area, expect a final price on the high side of the range—it could be *much* more.

Ways to Save Opt for a DJ—they almost always cost less than a band. Stay away from Saturday, since the best DJs and bands are in highest demand on Saturday nights—try Friday or Sunday for a slightly discounted rate. Keep it small—a four- or five-piece group will cost less than a fourteen-member orchestra complete with vocalist (and if the band's equipment is up-to-date, a smaller combo shouldn't sound like it's *that* much smaller).

Think of Your Guests Maybe you love hip-hop, but what about Grandma and Grandpa? Be sure the band or DJ can play some Sinatra and Cole Porter standards, too.

Size It Up Consider the size of your reception room and your crowd. An intimate space is not going to fit Jerry Jones & His Orchestra. A three-piece combo may not cut it for a guest list of four hundred. A good rule of thumb: six pieces per hundred people.

MC for Me If you want the bandleader or DJ to announce the wedding party and the events of the reception, be sure he or she has the necessary information. Write down all names (with pronunciations), roles, and relation to you (mother, best friend, and so on). More important, if you *don't* want the entertainment to an-nounce things, make sure they know that, too. (Do remember that you will need someone to announce when you want your guests to head to the buffet, but that can be done table by table by your banquet manager.)

Give 'em a Break Expect the entertainment to write breaks into their contract; there may even be union rules requiring that they take them. Have the bandleader or DJ arrange for recorded background music during intermissions.

Go for Five If you think your reception is going to go long, consider hiring the band or DJ for five hours instead of the typical four. It'll probably be cheaper than the overtime fees you'd incur if you decide on the spot to have them stay longer.

Beware the Pair Some DJs work with a partner—one person spins the tunes and the other serves as MC and/or gets the crowd pumped. Make sure everyone you hire understands the style you're looking for, and make sure to meet the person who will MC.

How Special Find out if your band or DJ uses any special equipment (lasers or strobe lights, bubble machine, fog generator), and make it known if you don't want certain kinds of props used.

Hiring the Ceremony & Cocktail Hour Musicians Checklist

☐ Book your favorite musicians by phone. Fax to confirm; include your wedding date.

☐ Finalize decisions as to:

Instrument(s) to be played _____

Music to be sung or played:

    Prelude _____

    _____

    _____

    Processional _____

    During ceremony _____

    Recessional _____

    Postlude _____

    During cocktail hour _____

    _____

☐ Request a contract or letter of agreement and review for the following critical points:
- Name and contact information for you and the vendor
- Your wedding date, address of location, and exact arrival time
- The name(s) of, and the instrument(s) played by, the musician(s)
- Any equipment you or the site will supply
- The names of the selections to be played
- Any agreements for you to supply sheet music
- What the musician(s) will wear
- The number of hours the musician(s) will play
- Total price
- Deposit amount due
- Balance and date due
- Cancellation and refund policy
- Musician's signature

☐ Sign final contract.

Hiring the Reception Band or DJ Checklist

☐ Ask for a tape of each band's live music, or a video of a DJ performing (but don't make your decision based solely on tapes). Ask if it's possible to see each band or DJ in action (you may be able to poke your head into another reception).

☐ When you see each band or DJ perform, notice:
- Stage presence/voice
- Interaction with the crowd
- Whether the music is continuous and/or has smooth transitions
- If the band or DJ seems comfortable/in control

☐ Call references and ask:
- Did the crowd enjoy themselves? Did people dance?
- Did the band or DJ play most of the songs on their playlist?
- Did the correct musicians show up at the event, as expected?

☐ Book your favorite band or DJ by phone. Send a fax to confirm.

☐ Finalize decisions as to:

If a band, how many musicians, and what instruments _____

_____

☐ Music to be sung or played:

First dance _____

Father/daughter _____

Mother/son _____

Last dance _____

☐ Request a contract and review for the following critical points:
- Name and contact information for you and the vendor
- Your wedding date, address of location, and exact arrival time
- Whether the bandleader or DJ will also serve as MC
- The number of hours the band or DJ will work
- Any equipment you or the site needs to supply—chairs, tables, music stands, amplifiers
- Equipment the band or DJ will supply
- Must-play songs (or date by which you need to supply song list)
- Any songs you definitely *don't* want played
- Any agreements for you to supply CDs or sheet music
- What the musicians or DJ will wear
- Total price
- Overtime rate, should your reception run long
- Deposit amount due
- Balance and date due
- Cancellation and refund policy
- Bandleader or DJ's signature

☐ Sign final contract.

staple business card here

CONTACT CHEAT SHEET:
Ceremony Musicians

Names: _____

Address: _____

_____

Contact: _____

Phone: _____

E-mail: _____

Fax: _____

Web site: _____

Estimate $ _____

Deposit $ _____   Date paid: ____ /____ /____

Total cost $ _____

Balance $ _____   Date due: ____ /____ /____

Notes

_____
_____
_____
_____
_____
_____
_____
_____
_____
_____
_____
_____
_____
_____
_____
_____
_____

CONTACT CHEAT SHEET:
Cocktail Hour Musicians

Names: _____

Address: _____

_____

Contact: _____

Phone: _____

E-mail: _____

Fax: _____

Web site: _____

Estimate $ _____

Deposit $ _____   Date paid: ____ / ____ / ____

Total cost $ _____

Balance $ _____   Date due: ____ / ____ / ____

staple business card here

Notes

_____

_____

_____

_____

_____

_____

_____

_____

_____

_____

_____

_____

_____

_____

_____

_____

staple business card here

CONTACT CHEAT SHEET:
Reception Musicians/DJ

Band or DJ name: _____

Address: _____

_____

Contact: _____

Phone: _____

E-mail: _____

Fax: _____

Web site: _____

Estimate $ _____

Deposit $ _____   Date paid: ____ / ____ / ____

Total cost $ _____

Balance $ _____   Date due: ____ / ____ / ____

Notes

_____

_____

_____

_____

_____

_____

_____

_____

_____

_____

_____

_____

_____

_____

_____

_____

bridesmaids' dresses

M ost bridesmaids' dresses these days are more than bearable: many are downright flatter-ing. Start shopping for your maids' gowns as soon as you've decided on your dress. Take at least one attendant with you when you shop—you'll need her as an advocate. It will take a few months to coordinate sizes, for the dresses to come in, and for alterations. Start as soon after the seven-month mark as you can.

Bridesmaids' Fashion Worksheet

Style

☐ Formal   ☐ Informal
☐ Traditional   ☐ Trendy
☐ Long sleeves   ☐ Short sleeves or sleeveless
☐ Floor-length   ☐ Tea-length or shorter
☐ One-piece   ☐ Mix-and-match pieces
☐ Ornate, beaded   ☐ Simple, unadorned

Coordination

☐ Identical styles
☐ Different style for honor attendant
☐ Each attendant chooses her own style

Accessories

☐ Wraps   ☐ Gloves
☐ Purses   ☐ Jewelry

Colors

_____

_____

_____

Budget per dress (consult bridesmaids) $ _____

Calling All Dress Shops

Research stores (the salon where you bought or shopped for your wedding gown, a wedding warehouse or outlet-type store, the dress department of your favorite department store) and ask bridesmaids for any "off-limits" styles or colors. The best place to get a sense of all the styles out there is **www.theknot.com/bridalsearch**.

Make appointments at several salons (preferably the one you are already working with):

Name: _____

Address: _____

_____

Phone: _____

Referred by: _____

App't date: ___ /___/ ___ Time: _____

Notes: _____

_____

_____

_____

Name: _____

Address: _____

_____

Phone: _____

Referred by: _____

App't date: ___ /___/ ___ Time: _____

Notes: _____

_____

_____

_____

Favorite designers and styles

_____

_____

_____

_____

_____

_____

_____

_____

Questions to Ask Dress Shops

☐ Which designers' dresses is the store authorized to carry? Can you get designers' catalogs?

☐ What size sample dresses are available to try on?

☐ Are there color-swatch charts, so you can see what colors different styles are available in?

☐ Can you and your bridesmaids look through the dresses yourselves, or are they shown by a salesperson?

☐ How long does it generally take for the dresses to come in after they've been ordered? (Average is one to two months.)

☐ Can the order be rushed, if necessary?

☐ If you ordered your wedding dress through the same store, will your bridesmaids (or you) be offered a discount or free alterations?

Knot Knowledge: Bridesmaid Dress Tips

What It Costs Anywhere from $50 to $400 per dress, depending on the designer and where you shop, but the average is $150 to $250. Bridesmaids should factor in an additional $50 for alterations and another $50 to $75 for shoes.

Get Everyone's Input Make sure everyone sees the dress (even if it's just a picture) and okays the style before you order.

Viva Variety Don't make your bridesmaids wear the exact same dress. Choose a designer, choose a color, and let them each make their own choice from the line.

Color-Coordinate If you are dead set on matching maids, it's a good idea to order all the dresses at the same store so that they'll be created from the same batch of fabric. (Same goes for dyeing shoes.)

Chip in If You Can While it's not required, we think it's nice to pay for part—if not all—of the dress, particularly if your taste is extravagant.

Custom Maid If you can't all agree or your maids are more concerned about the style(s) they wear than you are, buy fabric and then hook them up with a seamstress—they can design their own dresses.

Shop Till You Drop You aren't bound to shop in a bridal salon. Off-the-rack at your favorite chain store will do, too. Make sure everyone buys the dress ASAP once you find it, though, because retail is not as accommodating as custom.

Hair Care Don't inform your attendants they *must* get their hair professionally done (and pay for it themselves) on wedding day. Make it a gift from you, or let them do their own hair.

Black Is Back A bridal party in black is your best (and, frankly, easiest) option for an evening affair. Nobody can complain about the color—and who can't use another black dress? All-white (or ivory) bridal parties are also all the rage.

Bridesmaid Dress Etiquette & Issues

Q: How do I tell my bridesmaids that they have to pay for their own dresses? Two of them have never been in a wedding before.

A: The fact that they haven't been in a wedding before should actually make it easy—they don't know any different, right? Just explain that when someone stands up in a wedding, they are responsible for paying for what they'll wear. If you think cost is going to be an issue, do all you can to choose a dress that's reasonably priced—or consider letting the attendants choose their own dresses, so they'll get to decide how much to spend.

Q: Do the bridesmaids' dresses need to coordinate with what the groomsmen wear?

A: Your wedding party's outfits should have the same level of formality—for example, if your maids are wearing casual summer sundresses, the guys can't be in tuxes. Beyond that, if the guys will wear cummerbunds or vests, you'll probably want to choose a color that complements the bridesmaids' dresses. Often the men's only color is in their boutonnieres—and since those flowers will likely complement the bride's bouquet (and by association the bridesmaids' flowers), everyone should match.

Q: How closely do the bridesmaids' dresses have to match the bride's gown?

A: Generally, the attendants should wear dresses that match the formality of the bride's dress. You wouldn't want to put the maids in sundresses when the bride's in a formal gown, but as far as the actual style of the dress and the details (neckline, sleeves, and other elements), they do not have to match exactly, if at all.

Q: A few of my attendants are cranky because they don't like the dress I've chosen for them. Shouldn't they just wear what I want them to?

A: You stress about how you look in a dress, right? Why should your pals be any different? While it is almost impossible to make everyone 100 percent happy, you should still shoot for that. Be honest. Is your heart set on a sleek sheath dress you saw on a skinny model in a magazine, but your attendants are mostly curvy and not that tall? Did you choose sea foam simply because you want it to be your wedding color, without any regard to the fact that it makes most women look like freaks? Be sensitive to your attendants' varying body shapes and coloring. Ask their opinion, and be flexible.

Q: My matron of honor is pregnant, but it's really expensive to make alterations to the bridesmaid dress we picked out. Is it okay for her to wear a different style?

A: Not only is it okay, it's downright classy and cool. The best bet to accommodate her growing tummy: an empire-waist dress, with a high waistline (right under the bust) and a roomy A-line skirt that doesn't constrict hips, waist, or stomach.

Ordering the Bridesmaids' Dresses Checklist

☐ Along with your maids, decide on a dress (or several styles).

☐ Get measurements—bust, waist, and hips—from all bridesmaids (have out-of-towners send theirs to you).

☐ Decide what sizes to order. Ask to see the manufacturer's sizing chart yourself, and choose the size that fits each maid's largest measurement.

☐ Before you pay, review your receipt for the following critical points (bridesmaids may each do this separately; you may supervise orders for out-of-towners):
  - Name and contact information for you (or the bridesmaid) and the vendor
  - Your wedding date
  - A detailed description of the dress or dresses, including:
    Designer or manufacturer name(s)
    Style number(s)
    Size(s)
    Color(s)
    Fabric(s)
    Number of dresses ordered
  - Any special requests (different sleeves and so on)
  - Date the dresses will be delivered to the store
  - Descriptions of any accessories you order (for example, shoes to match)
  - Total price
  - Deposit amount due
  - Balance and date due
  - Cancellation and refund policy
  - Salesperson's signature

☐ Sign and keep receipt.

Bridesmaids' Alterations & Accessories Checklist

☐ Based on when the dresses are expected to come in, have all local bridesmaids schedule a fitting.

☐ About a month after ordering, call the shop to reconfirm delivery date.

☐ When the dresses arrive, you or the maid of honor should go see them to make sure they are the style(s) you ordered and that nothing is damaged.

☐ Have maid of honor pick up out-of-towners' gowns (she'll likely have to pay the balance; ask the other attendants to reimburse her, or you) and ship them to each maid. They should have fittings done at a tailor's or dress shop near them.

☐ Shop for and choose a shoe style. Let your bridesmaids know where to get them, or purchase them yourself and send them out. (Or just give them guidelines and let them choose their own shoes.)

☐ Touch base with all maids to be sure they pick up their fitted gowns and pay the balance.

Bridesmaids' Measurements & Fittings Checklist

Name: _____

Measurements: Bust _____   Waist _____   Hips _____

☐ Has dress   ☐ Fitting _____ / _____ / _____

Name: _____

Measurements: Bust _____   Waist _____   Hips _____

☐ Has dress   ☐ Fitting _____ / _____ / _____

Name: _____

Measurements: Bust _____   Waist _____   Hips _____

☐ Has dress   ☐ Fitting _____ / _____ / _____

Name: _____

Measurements: Bust _____   Waist _____   Hips _____

☐ Has dress   ☐ Fitting _____ / _____ / _____

Name: _____

Measurements: Bust _____   Waist _____   Hips _____

☐ Has dress   ☐ Fitting _____ / _____ / _____

Name: _____

Measurements: Bust _____   Waist _____   Hips _____

☐ Has dress   ☐ Fitting _____ / _____ / _____

Name: _____

Measurements: Bust _____   Waist _____   Hips _____

☐ Has dress   ☐ Fitting _____ / _____ / _____

Name: _____

Measurements: Bust _____   Waist _____   Hips _____

☐ Has dress   ☐ Fitting _____ / _____ / _____

CONTACT CHEAT SHEET:
Bridesmaid Dress Shop

(You may want to give each
bridesmaid her own copy of this sheet.)

staple business card here

Name: _____

Address: _____

_____

Contact: _____

Phone: _____

Fax: _____

Web site: _____

Store hours: _____

Dress description(s) and style number(s): _____

Date dresses will be in:_____ /_____ /_____

Deposit $_____   Date paid: ____ /____ /____

Total cost $_____

Balance $_____   Date due: ____ /____ /____

Notes

_____

_____

_____

_____

_____

_____

_____

_____

_____

_____

_____

_____

_____

_____

Notes

photography

If you're going to splurge on anything for your wedding, it should be the pictures. They'll preserve your memories better than anything else you purchase for the big event. And because the photographer you choose is going to capture your day minute by minute, you'll want to feel comfortable with this person. Rapport is important with all wedding professionals, but it's crucial here!

Wedding Photos Worksheet

Style and Film

- ☐ Traditional (posed shots and formal portraits)
- ☐ Photo journalism (coverage of events as they happen)
- ☐ Combination
- ☐ Black & white
- ☐ Color
- ☐ Both: _____% color, _____% b/w
- ☐ Digital

Subjects to be covered

- ☐ Prewedding preparations
- ☐ Ceremony
- ☐ Reception
- ☐ Formal/group portraits
- ☐ Bride/groom portraits
- ☐ _____

Final product

- ☐ Wedding album(s) #_____
- ☐ Insert-style album
- ☐ Bound album
- ☐ Loose prints
- ☐ Presentation box

Photography budget $_____

Calling All Photographers

To find photographers, ask friends with fantastic wedding pictures or get recommendations from caterers, florists, or consultants. Check out **www.TheKnot.com/local** to find local photographers (you can also look at their work for the many real weddings there).

Make appointments with several photographers:

Name: _____   Name: _____

Address: _____   Address: _____

_____   _____

Phone:_____   Phone:_____

Web site: _____   Web site: _____

Referred by: _____   Referred by: _____

App't date: ___ /___/___ Time: _____   App't date: ___ /___/___ Time: _____

Price estimate: $_____   Price estimate: $_____

Notes: _____   Notes: _____

_____   _____

_____   _____

_____   _____

_____   _____

Questions to Ask Photographers

- [ ] What's the photographer's primary style—traditional posed shots and portraits or photojournalism? (You must see their work to know the real answer to this question.)

- [ ] What is his or her philosophy about shooting weddings? (This will give you an idea of the person's expertise and passion for his or her work, too.)

- [ ] Does the photographer shoot in color, black and white, or both?

- [ ] Does the photographer shoot film or digitally?

- [ ] How independent is the photographer? Does he or she prefer that you describe exactly what you want, or would he or she rather be given free rein to capture the festivities on film in the way he or she sees fit? (This is a matter of how you two will work together.)

- [ ] Will the photographer you talk to be the one taking the pictures at your wedding? (This is crucial! Each photographer's style is his or her own.)

- [ ] Has the photographer done many weddings? (A photographer who doesn't specialize in weddings is a risk. You want someone who's experienced with how a wedding works so that key moments aren't missed.)

- [ ] Will the photographer be shooting any other wedding on your wedding day? (You don't want them to have any time constraints.)

- [ ] Is he or she open to a list of must-take photos (the people whom you definitely want shots of)?

- [ ] How does the photographer determine price? Is it by the number and kind of prints you think you'll want, the hours the photographer works your wedding, developing time, a combination of all of these? Are there packages available? Can you get a price list?

- [ ] How will you first be shown photos? (Options are: contact sheets, numbered proofs [small photos], CD-ROM, videotape, in-studio slide show, or on the photographer's Web site.)

- [ ] What kind of lighting and other equipment (such as tripods) does the photographer use? Does he/she bring along backup equipment in case of an emergency?

- [ ] Does the photographer develop his or her own film? How long does he/she keep negatives? Can you buy your negatives from the photographer?

Photography Etiquette

Q: I love the look of photojournalistic wedding photography, but all my married friends have traditional, posed pictures. How do I decide?

A: Ideally, you'll want a mix of posed and spontaneous images. While all photographers promise a mix of the two styles, they will inevitably gravitate toward one style. So if you adore the idea of documentary-style images, you'll probably want to hire someone who specializes in a more photojournalistic style. Then, simply discuss which posed shots you'd also like. It's harder for a portrait photographer to do the reverse.

Q: When should formal pictures be taken?

A: It's up to you. Here are the options:

- *Before the ceremony.* Our favorite! Of course, if you want to uphold the tradition of not seeing each other before the wedding, this is out. But more and more couples choose to spend time alone prior to the ceremony, and it's a great opportunity to get family and wedding-party portraits done when everyone's excited and fresh.
- *After the ceremony.* The newlyweds and wedding party take pictures while guests wait outside or travel to the reception and start the cocktail hour. (So as not to make guests wait for hours, keep the list to the bare minimum: couple alone, with parents, with wedding party, with bride's family, and with groom's family.)
- *During the reception.* Some couples steal away to take shots with their wedding party and families. Consider whether you want to take this time away from your guests. And beware—you won't look as fresh.
- *Afterward.* You might have to redo your makeup! It definitely depends on how late the party will go, too. The biggest advantage: absolutely no distractions or nerves.

Q: We're on a really tight budget. How smart is it to hire a photography student or ask a guest who's an amateur photographer to take pictures?

A: If you find a truly talented student, or if you've always admired your cousin's skill as a shutterbug, this might be an option. Just keep in mind that if the person doesn't have wedding experience, you might not get the results you want. Honestly, you'll probably do better trying to save elsewhere.

Q: I'm concerned that my photographer won't get shots of all the guests I want. How do I make sure this happens without being a total control freak?

A: Take the responsibility off your shoulders by giving him or her a list of must-take photos in advance—certain moments and/or people that you definitely want captured on film. Ask a relative or close friend to be on call to point out specific people for the photographer. An interesting idea we saw recently: A backdrop was set up in a corner of the reception room, and anyone interested could go over in groups for shots with the bride and groom. This was an easy way for groups of family and friends to take the responsibility into their own hands.

Q: Color or black-and-white film—which to choose?

A: There's definitely a trend back toward black-and-white wedding pictures. There's something dramatic and timeless about photographs in shades of only black, white, and gray. But with color film, you'll capture all the details you so painstakingly planned. Your best bet (and our preference): a combination of the two, with a leaning toward black-and-white.

Q: What are the benefits of having our photographer shoot digitally?

A: Digital cameras do not use film—they record the visual information of a picture in an entirely electronic form. The advantages of digital photography are cost (no film development costs), archiving (no "negatives"; all of your "negatives" with digital photography can be kept on CDs), and ease of sharing (you can easily e-mail your friends and family wedding photos without having to scan the prints). Photographers may charge more (especially if they need to rent a camera), but it may save you money in the long run.

What It Costs A basic package can cost $2,000, but a quality photographer begins closer to $3,000. You're paying for the photographer's time at the wedding, plus the hours spent developing your pictures, plus the prints and albums you order. If your photographer is in high demand, expect to pay dearly (more than $7,000, even way above) for the honor of his or her presence!

Ways to Save Hire your photographer for a limited amount of time—just the ceremony and an hour at the reception, perhaps. Keep prints simple; special developing treatments such as sepia tones or complicated printing techniques cost more because they take more darkroom work. A photographer who views his or her work as art may charge more than a large studio with multiple photographers that functions more as a wedding-photo factory. Go solo—photographers who work with assistants will probably cost more. Choose a package carefully. For example, some may include parents' albums, but many don't, which means you may pay an additional fee later.

Call the Shots Ask recently married friends how many pictures their photographer took (that is, how many proofs they got) and whether the number was sufficient, so you'll have a frame of reference when talking to your photographer. At an average wedding (ceremony and four-hour reception), a traditional photographer shoots about three hundred exposures; a photojournalistic photographer will shoot anywhere from five hundred to one thousand.

See an Actual Album Look at pictures from a previous wedding the photographer shot to see if he or she connected to the couple and really captured their day. If possible, also ask to see a proof book—the shots the photographer took before the couple chose the ones they wanted. This is his or her work in the raw.

Beware the Bait and Switch Some contracts spell out the studio's right to send any staff photographer to your wedding—don't sign if that's not okay with you.

Don't Underestimate You may not think you need a lot of pictures, but chances are you'll want more than you thought once you see them (especially if you've hired a spectacular photographer). Err on the side of more prints.

Negatives Are Positive Most professional photographers keep their own negatives—you'll get the best-quality prints, and negatives will be properly stored. Have them kept on file with your photographer for as long as that person has a policy of keeping them; you may then be able to buy them yourselves.

Let Guests in on It If you order prints for family and friends, be sure everyone knows the price per print—or prepare to tack additional fees onto your final tab! Order parents' and guests' prints at the same time as your own to avoid reorder fees.

Album Options Photographers' albums can get pricey. Make sure to ask who designs the layout (you, them, a combination), whether all pages have full-size prints (a variety is more interesting), and whether both black-and-white and color prints are included. If you buy your own, be careful not to use a cheap album—it may damage your pictures over time.

Get Behind the Scenes Choose a photo pro you feel extremely comfortable about inviting backstage. Some of the most beautiful wedding moments are those that happen while the bride is dressing, where the family is waiting, or when the couple steals away for a kiss.

ERICKA & ERIC: A WELL-PHOTOGRAPHED EVENT

October 4
Glen Ellen, CA
Planning Time Frame: 9 months

AS A PROFESSIONAL PHOTOGRAPHER HERSELF, Ericka was totally focused on her own wedding pictures. She had many talented colleagues, and it was important to her to hire a photographer whose work she knew well. Then one bestowed a gift. "Philippe Cheng, an incredible photographer and a very good friend, offered to shoot our wedding as his present to us," Ericka says. "I love him and his images so much that it was an easy decision." His wife, Bastienne, also a photographer, would shoot as well.

"Philippe's and Bastienne's visions are amazing. The moments they caught between me and Eric are so tender and loving, they completely catch the emotion of the day," Ericka says. The couple's comfort level with Philippe and Bastienne was crucial to the great pictures that resulted. "They were around the entire time—behind the scenes with us when we were getting ready, and they also stole us away from the party when the light was right."

Philippe shot not only stills, but also some video—an extra bonus, and not intrusive at all, Ericka says. "We decided not to hire a professional videographer, because we had been to weddings where the video person was so aggressive that it made people really uptight," she explains. "Still, it was great to have some moving images. We got to see everything we missed, like people having fun and who talked to whom."

Ericka and Eric's Photography Tips

- Talk about your vision with your photographer. Make sure they know what and who is important to you.
- The photographer's style is as important as his or her personality. "It's great if you like the person, but really you should like their style, because that's what you're going to get," Ericka says.
- If you're having an evening wedding, ask to see examples of nighttime photography. Make sure the photographer can do what you want.
- Have a great time—it will show in your photos!

Hiring the Photographer Checklist

☐ Carefully examine samples of each photographer's past work (his or her "book"). Be sure you're looking at work he or she shot, not that of other professionals who work at the same studio.

☐ Notice whether:
- Photos are framed well
- Photos are over- or underexposed
- Details are visible
- People look comfortable and relaxed

☐ Call references and ask:
- Did the photographer get the shots they expected and wanted?
- Were they satisfied overall?

☐ Book your favorite photographer by phone, send a fax to confirm.

☐ Finalize decisions as to:

The specific package you're purchasing (if applicable) _____

Percentage posed vs. photojournalistic _____

How much film will be shot (including color/b&w ratio) _____

If shooting digital, how many CDs will be expected _____

How many proofs you'll have to choose from _____

How much time will be needed for posed, formal portraits _____

☐ Request a contract and review for the following critical points:
- Name and contact information for you and the vendor
- Date, exact times (number of hours), and locations (home, ceremony, reception) where the photographer will work on wedding day
- The name of the photographer who will be shooting your wedding and the number and names of assistants
- That there will be backup gear available
- Number of rolls of film to be shot (color and black and white), as well as type of film (and cost per additional roll, if needed)
- Number of proofs you'll receive, and other package details if you opt for one (you may modify this information later)
- The date your proofs will be ready and how long you can keep them
- When you'll receive your order (albums, prints) once you place it
- Length of time the photographer will keep your negatives
- Total cost (itemized if possible)
- Overtime fees
- Reorder price, if you should decide to order additional pictures later
- Deposit amount due
- Balance and date due
- Cancellation and refund policy
- Photographer's signature

☐ Sign final contract.

CONTACT CHEAT SHEET:
Photographer

Name: _____

Address: _____

_____

Contact: _____

Phone: _____

Fax: _____

E-mail: _____

Details of photography package: _____

_____

_____

Estimate $_____

Deposit $_____   Date paid: ____ / ____ / ____

Total cost $_____

Balance $_____   Date due: ____ / ____ / ____

Notes

_____

_____

_____

_____

_____

_____

_____

_____

_____

_____

_____

_____

_____

staple business card here

Notes

videography

Many brides and grooms say that their wedding was over before they knew it, and they feel like they missed a lot of what went on. Video technology today makes it possible for weddings to be filmed quite unobtrusively. Since photographers and videographers work together quite closely, you'll probably want to hire these professionals at about the same time; you may even want to ask your photographer (whom you should hire first) for a referral.

Wedding Video Worksheet

Style
- ☐ Unedited footage
- ☐ Multiple cameras (better coverage)
- ☐ Special effects (pictures, voice-overs, music, titling)
- ☐ Tightly edited
- ☐ One camera (unobtrusive)
- ☐ Unconventional composition and lighting

Elements to be filmed/footage to be included
- ☐ Prewedding preparations
- ☐ Ceremony
- ☐ Reception
- ☐ Guest interviews
- ☐ Home videos

Special considerations: _____

Videography budget $_____

Video Etiquette & Issues

Q: If we already have a photographer, do we need a videographer, too?

A: It's up to you. A photographer should come first, but video has a completely different feel. Because it's in real time, and living color—and you can include pictures from your pasts and courtship, music important to you, and guest interviews—a video is a very full and emotional way to preserve your wedding memories.

Q: What should a good videographer include for the price of a package?

A: Whether you choose bare-bones coverage or all the bells and whistles, any videographer should supply the following: backup camera(s), lights, batteries, wireless microphones (if you want them used)—and courtesy to guests. You can also expect interesting shots and creative and entertaining coverage of your day. One of the most important reasons for hiring a professional to videotape your wedding, besides his or her expertise, is the ability to edit a video smoothly. Every package should include at least one edited tape.

Q: Does the couple have any say about how the tape is edited?

A: When you're interviewing videographers, ask about this. Some may let you watch the raw footage (or a loosely edited reel) and decide what you want left in (the entire ceremony, the wedding party's entrance, the first dance, and so on) or taken out (off-color remarks by guests, friends, and relatives; the bride captured doing embarrassing things). Others may let you give them a general idea of what you want left in and taken out and will do the editing themselves.

Q: Are certain venues more conducive than others to videography?

A: Weddings *not* held in a house of worship are often better in terms of videography. Outdoor weddings, in a park or backyard, can give the cameraperson more freedom. Weddings held in a banquet hall or hotel allow the videographer to set up in the best locations and get the shots the bride and groom want. Basically, the less traditional the setting for the wedding, the more liberty the videographer has.

Calling All Videographers

Your photographer and site manager are your best sources for finding good videographers. Also, ask recently married friends who had good experiences and whose videos you've seen and liked.

Set up appointments with several videographers:

Name: _____

Address: _____

_____

Phone: _____

Referred by: _____

App't date: ___ / ___ / ___ Time: _____

Price estimate: $_____

Notes: _____

_____

_____

_____

_____

_____

Name: _____

Address: _____

_____

Phone: _____

Referred by: _____

App't date: ___ / ___ / ___ Time: _____

Price estimate: $_____

Notes: _____

_____

_____

_____

_____

_____

Questions to Ask Videographers

☐ What's the videographer's style—artsy, documentary, or direct (doing interviews with guests)? Does this jibe with what you want?

☐ Has the videographer done many weddings? What's his or her approach when it comes to taping a wedding? (This clues you in to experience and philosophy.)

☐ Has the videographer worked with your photographer before? How does he or she coordinate with a wedding photographer? (This is really important!)

☐ Has this person ever shot a wedding at your ceremony and/or reception site? If so, can you see that tape?

☐ How many other weddings is the videographer doing on your wedding day or weekend? (Make sure there are no time constraints.)

☐ Will the videographer you're speaking to be the one who will shoot your wedding?

☐ What kind, how many, and how new are the cameras, tapes, and microphones the videographer uses? (Can you get a DVD instead of a video?)

☐ If you want editing, ask about the equipment the tape will be edited on. (Typically, a digital video-editing system will produce the most professional-looking video, but it depends on the quality of the equipment itself.)

☐ How obtrusive are the shooting style and the crew? How bright are the lights they use? (If the shooting requires the room lights to be on all evening, much of the romance may be lost.)

☐ How does the videographer charge? Are there packages? Ask for a price list.

Knot Knowledge: Video Tips & Trends

What It Costs On average, hiring a videographer will cost $1,000 to $2,000, but it can be less or more depending on where you live, how many camerapeople you hire, and the complexity of the editing (if any).

Ways to Save Consider having only the ceremony filmed. Forgo complicated editing (but you'll want at least minimal editing to make the tape more watchable—otherwise you'll end up with four to eight hours of loose video, some of which is not so interesting). Opt for a single camera. Forget special effects such as animated titles or still photos.

Ask Before You Shoot Some houses of worship forbid video. Others may restrict the videographer to a certain space.

Keep It Low-Key Don't settle for huge, unruly equipment and blinding lights. Modern video technology should not require floodlights and is often smaller and easier to handle than in the past. Remember, though, that very low light in the space overall will lead to less-than-perfect video. Alert your space manager and have him or her discuss light levels with the videographer.

Make It Memorable Give the videographer snapshots of the two of you during your dating days or honeymoon, favorite songs, newspaper clippings, and anything else that might add dimension to your edited video.

Keep It Short No one (except maybe your mom) wants to spend four hours watching your wedding video. Keep the edited tape around an hour long and subject only yourselves to watching the unedited footage. Also, try to get an even shorter, 10-minute version—a "highlights" reel to show less-obsessed friends and family.

Double Trouble If you hire your photographer and videographer separately, ask that they meet before the wedding to coordinate shooting styles and strategies. If they have worked together before, that can be a bonus. But don't assume that their quality will be the same; interview each professional separately. If you're pressured to hire them as a team and it makes you uncomfortable, go elsewhere.

Be Heard Discuss where and how you will be miked for the ceremony; also make sure it's okay with your officiant. Without mikes, you won't hear the vows on the tape.

If You Ask a Friend . . . The quality of tape from a consumer camera will be different (think home movie vs. professional documentary), and the person may not have the editing skill of a professional. Still, this is a good option if you have no budget or aren't interested in a full film crew.

Copyright Law Counts A professional DVD or videotape is just like a rental—copying it is illegal. Most packages include at least one edited tape or DVD. Order a few extra to pass around—very few people need one for forever.

Don't Tape Over It When you receive your video, break off the safety tab on the back immediately so you don't accidentally tape over your wedding.

Hiring the Videographer Checklist

☐ Watch a few tapes from past weddings. Notice whether:
- The images are clear (not out of focus)
- The lighting is right (not too dim or too harsh)
- Sound quality is good.
- If the tape was edited, the cuts are smooth
- If special effects were added, they look professional

☐ Call references and ask:
- Was the videographer a pleasant presence at their wedding?
- Did the videographer capture the most important aspects of their wedding?
- Were they happy overall?

☐ Book your favorite videographer by phone, send a fax to confirm.

☐ Finalize decisions as to:

What (ceremony, reception, or both) will be taped _____

The components of the package you're purchasing (if applicable) _____

_____

Special requests (people and events your videographer must catch, songs or

pictures to use in editing) _____

_____

_____

☐ Request a contract and review for the following critical points:
- Name and contact information for you and the vendor
- Date, exact times (number of hours), and locations (home, ceremony, reception) where the videographer will work on wedding day
- Name of the videographer(s) who will be shooting your wedding, as well as the number of assistants
- Number and kind(s) of cameras to be used
- Number of videos and DVDs you'll receive, and complete package details (specifics of special editing and so on)
- Date your unedited video will be ready
- Date you'll receive your finished, edited video
- Total cost, with all charges itemized
- Overtime fee, if applicable
- Reorder prices, if you should decide to order additional videos later
- Deposit amount due
- Balance and date due
- Cancellation and refund policy
- Videographer's signature

☐ Sign final contract.

CONTACT CHEAT SHEET:
Videographer

Name: _____

staple business card here

Address: _____

_____

Contact: _____

Phone: _____

Fax: _____

Web site: _____

Details of videography package: _____

_____

Estimate $_____

Deposit $_____   Date paid: ____ / ____ / ____

Total cost $_____

Balance $_____   Date due: ____ / ____ / ____

Notes

_____
_____
_____
_____
_____
_____
_____
_____
_____
_____
_____
_____
_____
_____
_____
_____
_____

Notes

CHAPTER THIRTEEN

honeymoon

You can start planning your honeymoon as soon as you're engaged, and serious booking of your trip should happen five to six months before your wedding. Start right away if you're planning a foreign excursion, a complicated itinerary that takes you to several destinations, or a trip to a popular island or resort. Bon voyage!

Vacation Vision Worksheet

Style ☐ Beach getaway   ☐ Historical tour   ☐ Single location
☐ Urban escape   ☐ Lots of lounging   ☐ Multipart trip
☐ Exotic adventure   ☐ Lots of action

Location
☐ Foreign   ☐ In nature   ☐ Seaside
☐ Domestic   ☐ Urban   ☐ Combination

Accommodations   ☐ Deluxe resort   ☐ All-inclusive
☐ Intimate hotel   ☐ Pay-as-you-go

Length # _____ days/weeks

Departure

☐ Directly from wedding

(Date: _____ / _____ / _____ Earliest time: _____)

☐ Next day

(Date: _____ / _____ / _____ Earliest time: _____)

☐ Later date

(Date: _____ / _____ / _____ Earliest time: _____)

Dream destinations: _____

_____

_____

_____

Honeymoon budget $_____

ASK CARLEY
Honeymoon Etiquette

Q: Who's supposed to pay for the honeymoon?

A: These days, most couples pay for their honeymoon themselves, but often parents or other close relatives offer to finance the trip (or part of the trip) as a wedding gift. Traditionally, the groom and his family paid for the honeymoon because the bride's family financed the entire wedding. But modern wedding spending is more egalitarian, and just as you should not expect your parents to pop for the bash, you shouldn't expect them to pick up the tab for a three-week trip to Bali, either. It's likely that this is a gift you'll give yourselves.

Calling All Travel Agents

To find travel agents, ask friends to recommend professionals whom they've worked with successfully, or pinpoint someone who specializes in your destination of choice. Log onto **www.TheKnot.com/travel**.

Make appointments with several travel agents:

Name: _____   Name: _____

Address: _____   Address: _____

Phone: _____   Phone: _____

Referred by: _____   Referred by: _____

App't date: ___ /___/___ Time: _____   App't date: ___ /___/___ Time: _____

Notes: _____   Notes: _____

_____   _____

_____   _____

_____   _____

_____   _____

_____   _____

Questions to Ask Travel Agents

☐ What type of travel does the agent consider his or her specialty? (Make sure it's leisure, not business.) Any special focus in locales?

☐ Does the agent plan many honeymoons?

☐ Can he or she give you references—couples you can speak to whose honeymoons the agent planned?

☐ What are the agent's ideas, based on your constraints and interests?

☐ Has the agent personally been to the destinations or resorts he or she recommends? Are there brochures you can look at?

☐ Will the agent deliver all the items you need to travel (tickets, confirmations, maps), or do you need to come back in?

☐ If you need other documents (such as passports or visas for travel abroad), can the agent help arrange them?

☐ Is there a twenty-four-hour toll-free number in case of travel emergency?

Knot Knowledge: Honeymoon Tips

What It Costs Depending on how far you go and for how long, a honeymoon can cost anywhere from $1,000 to $8,000 (or more). Your total cost will include airfare (or train, bus, or carfare), hotel, ground transportation (taxis, etc.), food and drink, and souvenirs.

Ways to Save Stick close to home; if you can drive there, you can spend more on accommodations and activities. Use the frequent-flyer miles you earned using your trusty credit card to pay for wedding services. Avoid your destination's high season, the peak tourist time when things are most crowded and in demand. Check airfare out of nearby smaller cities—Milwaukee instead of Chicago, Baltimore instead of D.C. Go with a package instead of purchasing plane tickets, hotel, and food à la carte. Borrow a friend or relative's summer cottage or beach house.

Don't Forget Traveler's checks and/or your ATM card—check the newspaper or your bank for the current exchange rate (if you're traveling to a foreign country) right before you leave; your ID, passports, and other necessary paperwork; camera and film; comfortable shoes; dress-up clothes; bathing suits (even hotels in Alaska have swimming pools); birth control pills or other medication.

Be Safe If you're traveling to a third-world country or any politically unstable area, check the U.S. Department of State's Bureau of Consular Affairs advisories at 888-407-4747.

Stock Up at Home Buy last-minute stuff such as film and sunscreen before you leave. It's cheaper at the drugstore than at your destination.

Which Name for Passports? The bride's ticket, passport, and all other ID should be in her maiden name; if there are discrepancies, you could run into trouble in customs.

Spend a Night Nearby Don't feel as though you have to rush right off to your honeymoon. You'll have a much better first day in paradise if you get a good night's sleep in your wedding city first.

Honeymoon at Home If you can't travel right away, take at least two days off to celebrate privately and recuperate.

Expect to Be Blue Postwedding blues are natural. Embrace the feelings; talk about the wedding, and then enjoy your trip.

AMY & AMIR: A DOUBLE DREAM WEDDING

October 14 and November 17
La Quinta, CA, and
Tel Aviv, Israel
Planning Time Frame:
7 Months

AMY AND AMIR'S ROMANCE was nothing if not cosmopolitan. The couple met in graduate school in Arizona, then spent time together in Mexico, Toronto, and Atlanta before settling in New York City. They got engaged in February—on Amy's birthday—in Paris, her favorite city. With the groom's family in Israel, the bride's in California, and friends all over the world, the only way to have the wedding this couple truly wanted was to plan *two*. "It was important for us to celebrate both our cultures with all of our family and friends—especially because we don't live where they are," Amy says.

There was no time to waste. Amy and Amir wanted to wed that same fall, so, with the help of parents on both ends, they started looking for sites immediately, settling on the charming La Quinta Hotel in California, and Green Villa, an Arabic sheik's mansion dating from the early 1900s, in Tel Aviv. In May, the couple traveled to California for a whirlwind four days of planning—meeting with the hotel wedding coordinator, interviewing photographers and musicians, taste-testing wedding cakes, and securing an officiant. In August, they were off to Israel for a week, where they met with the videographer, photographer, and DJ; they also did a food tasting and purchased Amir's wedding suit. (Amy, who works for Carolina Herrera, was having a gown custom-designed for her in New York!) Everything fell into place, and this couple had two weddings to remember.

Amy and Amir's Two-Wedding Tips

- Alert guests early. "We let everyone know about our plans right after the engagement," Amy says. "And as soon as we set the dates, I let everyone know by June, so they could start planning the trip to one or both events."
- If you must, delay the honeymoon—but take one! Amy and Amir chose to spend their money and time on two amazing wedding locations and traveling to be with their closest family and friends. "I really think it's important to have one, though, to spend time alone and relax after all the hustle and bustle," Amy says.

Booking the Honeymoon Checklist

☐ Check references and make a final decision on your travel agent and your destination.

☐ Make hotel and air or train reservations (or have your travel agent arrange them). Ask about using frequent-flyer miles and/or special honeymoon hotel packages.

☐ If necessary, get passports, and ask the tourism bureau or your travel agent if you'll need other travel documents, such as visas.

☐ If your destination requires you to get immunizations, do so ASAP.

☐ Finalize or confirm travel and hotel reservations.

☐ Print out a copy of your itinerary.

Destination Wedding Tips

Choose Like Honeymooners Select your location with your honeymoon in mind (especially because it's probably going to be your honeymoon spot). Start by contacting the tourist board for the country or state you're thinking about.

Share the Plan Let potential guests know early, particularly if you choose a foreign country. Send accommodation and travel info ASAP. If you're flexible, find out what times might be good for them before you book your wedding date.

Play by the Rules If you're tying the knot in a foreign land, ask its tourism bureau or foreign consulate about the country's marriage requirements (minimum time you need to be in the country, fee, documents needed, and the like).

Wed Stress-Free Consider marrying at a resort with an on-site wedding consultant. Most will take care of everything for you, from the officiant to the cake.

Get There Early Finalize paperwork and details, meet with everyone who will be working on your wedding, and chill for a bit.

CONTACT CHEAT SHEET:
Travel Agent & Destination

Travel agent: _____

Address: _____

_____

Phone: _____

Emergency toll-free number: _____

Fax: _____

staple business card here

Destination: _____

Web sites: _____

_____

_____

_____

Tourism bureau number: _____

Foreign consulate number (in United States): _____

U.S. embassy number (if abroad): _____

Resort or hotel: _____

Address: _____

Contact: _____

Phone: _____ Fax: _____

Airline: _____ Flight numbers: _____

Toll-free number: _____

Travel dates: _____ / _____ / _____ to _____ / _____ / _____

Notes

_____

_____

_____

_____

Notes

flowers & decor

How much energy and time you devote to planning your wedding decor depends largely on your ceremony and reception sites: If they're already ornate, you'll need minimal decorations and flowers. If they're clean slates, you've got more work to do. If you want a full-service floral designer, you'll definitely want to book as soon as you've nailed down your wedding locations. If flowers and decor aren't critical to you, it's fine to book someone six months before the wedding.

Flowers & Ambiance Worksheet

Floral style

- ☐ Tightly arranged
- ☐ Natural-looking
- ☐ Minimalist
- ☐ Elaborate
- ☐ Subtle
- ☐ Striking

Flowers

- ☐ Seasonal or local blooms
- ☐ Exotic flowers
- ☐ Greens & herbs
- ☐ Berries & grasses

Favorite flowers _____

_____

Colors

- ☐ Monochromatic
- ☐ Multicolored
- ☐ Traditional (white, pastels)
- ☐ Modern (dark hues, citrus shades)

Favorite colors _____

_____

Floral needs

- ☐ Bridal bouquet/tossing bouquet
- ☐ Maid of honor's bouquet
- ☐ Bridesmaids' bouquets #_____
- ☐ Flower girl's flowers (or basket of petals)
- ☐ Corsages for moms and grandmothers #_____
- ☐ Groom's boutonniere
- ☐ Boutonnieres for groomsmen, ushers, dads, grandfathers #_____
- ☐ Altar arrangements #_____
- ☐ Flower-covered arch or huppah
- ☐ Rose petals for tossing
- ☐ Reception table centerpieces #_____
- ☐ Reception buffet table flowers
- ☐ Reception cake table flowers
- ☐ Additional greenery (such as potted plants)
- ☐ Door or doorway decorations

Other decorations

- ☐ Aisle runner
- ☐ Aisle decorations
- ☐ Fabric
- ☐ Lighting
- ☐ Furniture
- ☐ Balloons

Designer/florist budget $_____

Calling All Floral Designers

To find florists, ask newlywed friends or other wedding professionals: your caterer, photographer, wedding consultant, or banquet manager. Your bridal salon might be an especially good place—since flowers are the finishing touch to the bride's dress, they often work together closely. Also check with your officiant and/or the contact at your ceremony site. Check out **www.TheKnot.com/florists** for local flower pros, or visit local flower shops to see if you might want to approach them for your wedding.

Make appointments with several florists:

Name: _____   Name: _____

Address: _____   Address: _____

_____   _____

Phone: _____   Phone: _____

Web site: _____   Web site: _____

Referred by: _____   Referred by: _____

App't date: ___ /___/___ Time: _____   App't date: ___ /___/___ Time: _____

Price estimate: $_____   Price estimate: $_____

Notes: _____   Notes: _____

_____   _____

_____   _____

_____   _____

_____   _____

Questions to Ask Floral Designers

☐ Can you see photographs or live examples of past work? (Real bouquets and arrangements will give you a better idea than photos—especially photos that aren't of the florist's actual work but show things the florist says he or she *can* do.)

☐ Does the florist's style—and the overall look of the shop/studio—match yours? (This is common sense; you should get a good gut feeling.)

☐ Does the florist seem knowledgeable, offering suggestions for less expensive alternatives, the best flowers for the season in which your wedding will be held, and so on?

☐ Has the florist done weddings at your ceremony and/or reception sites before? (He or she may have pictures of arrangements done at your site, and he or she will be knowledgeable about what sizes, shapes, and colors work in the space.)

☐ If not, will she/he stop by prior to the wedding to check out the space?

☐ Will the florist simply drop flowers off for your wedding, or will he or she spend time at the sites, setting up and making sure everything is in order? (You'll pay for a full-service florist, but you get what you pay for.)

☐ How big is the shop (that is, number of staff), and who will ultimately be working on your wedding? (Make sure it's the floral designer with whom you discuss your vision.)

☐ How many weddings will the florist be doing on the same day or weekend as yours?

☐ Does the florist offer any rental items—vases, potted plants, arches, trellises, candelabras, urns? Or must you get these things from a rental company?

☐ Does the florist preserve bouquets? (If this is important to you, find out now if he or she will be able to do so after the wedding, or if you can be referred to someone who can. You may have to make an appointment *before* the wedding to ensure that your bouquet can be preserved directly afterward.)

Knot Knowledge: Floral Tips & Trends

What It Costs You could pay $900 or less if all you need are several personal arrangements. If you hire a full-service florist to create a blooming masterpiece, you can spend upward of $15,000. On average—personal flowers, a few nice ceremony and reception arrangements, and centerpieces for ten tables or so—you'll probably spend between $3,000 and $5,000.

Ways to Save The more complicated your arrangements, the more you'll spend; think simple and elegant. Stay in season. Easily acquired flowers will probably be less expensive. Choose built-in decor—if your reception site is a garden or is otherwise very ornate, you can use fewer flowers and still have a stunning room. A church will already be beautifully decorated for Christmas or Easter. On the other hand, roses (and florists) are in major demand (read: expensive) around Valentine's Day and Mother's Day. Focus on reception centerpieces and the bridal bouquet. Use rented potted plants instead of large floral arrangements; flowering plants rather than cut-flower centerpieces. Have bridesmaids lay their bouquets decoratively on the head table or cake table.

Have Faith Hire someone you trust to make the right floral decisions, someone who instinctively knows what will look good together. Don't obsess—as long as they're beautiful, who cares if the roses in the centerpieces are blush instead of pink?

Show, Don't Tell Bring a bridesmaid-dress fabric swatch and/or a photograph of your dress when you first see a florist. They'll help him or her understand your style.

Pick a Palette If color is the most important thing to you, just give your florist guidelines and let him or her choose the most affordable (and gorgeous) flowers available at the time of your wedding.

The Size Is Right Be sure they aren't too heavy, too fragrant, or too hard to carry—your bridesmaids will thank you.

Choose Hardy Blooms If your wedding will be in a very humid climate—especially if it's outside—certain flowers will wilt before you say your vows. Ask your florist which can withstand your weather.

Say Bouquet! Coordinate personal-flower delivery times with the arrival of the photographer—you'll want them to be worn or held in formal pictures.

Bloom Rules Ask your officiant if your ceremony site has any restrictions about floral decorations.

Go Wild Top floral designers are including elements such as herbs, berries, fruits, and grasses in arrangements. The look is modern, intriguing, and definitely worth a try.

Hiring the Floral Designer Checklist

☐ Ask each florist you're interested in to create a sample bouquet or arrangement for you.

☐ Have each florist put together a proposal for your wedding, based on what you've told him or her about your wedding vision and floral budget.

☐ Book your favorite florist by phone, send a fax to confirm.

☐ Finalize flower decisions—types, colors, and amounts:

Bouquets (bride and bridesmaids) _____

_____

Throwaway bouquet for the bouquet toss _____

Boutonnieres (groom, groomsmen, dads) _____

_____

Corsages (mothers, grandmothers) _____

_____

Floral head wreath (flower girl, bride) _____

_____

Ceremony arrangements (for around the altar or stage, lining the aisle, door wreaths) _____

_____

Huppah decorations, petals for guests to toss _____

_____

Reception arrangements (centerpieces, extra flowers for the head table, cake or cake-table flowers, arches over doors, any other room arrangements) _____

_____

_____

☐ Request a contract and review for the following critical points:
- Name and contact information for you and the vendor
- Date, times, and locations of your ceremony and reception
- An itemized list of all the flower arrangements you've chosen, from bouquets to centerpieces, including the names, colors, and amounts of each flower (you may modify this later when you've made final decisions)
- Flower alternatives should certain blooms be unavailable on your wedding day (also include anything unacceptable to you)
- A list of anything else the florist will supply—centerpiece vases, a trellis for the ceremony site, other accessories
- Arrival times and time needed for setup at the ceremony and reception sites

- Where and when bouquets and boutonnieres should be delivered (home, hotel, site—this information can be supplied at a later date if necessary)
- The name of the florist who will be on hand during the wedding
- Total cost (itemized if possible)
- Delivery and setup fees
- Deposit amount due
- Balance and date due
- Cancellation and refund policy
- Florist's signature

☐ Sign final contract.

Floral Etiquette

Q: How do we decide on flowers for the wedding party? And what about the groom's boutonniere—should it match the bride's bouquet?

A: The bride's bouquet is definitely the starting point for choosing personal flowers—all the other arrangements should complement hers. The bridesmaids' bouquets should echo the color and shape of the bride's but are usually smaller. They should also complement the color of the maids' dresses. The groom's boutonniere should be distinct from the groomsmen's somehow, perhaps with an extra bloom in a different color. It's nice if he wears a flower that's in the bride's bouquet as well. (Dads and grandfathers can wear boutonnieres to match the groomsmen.) Flower girls can carry mini bouquets that match the bridesmaids', wear a head wreath of blooms in the bride's bouquet, or carry a basket of petals or a pomander (a flower ball suspended on ribbon).

Q: Who should get corsages?

A: It's customary to give your mothers flowers—wrist corsages or something they can pin to their dresses, or even mini bouquets to carry. (If they are pinned corsages, make sure they're not such huge arrangements that they're hard to wear or damage clothing.) You may also decide to present your grandmothers with flowers, as well as any other special female relatives or close friends. It's also a nice gesture (and pretty much expected) to give stepmothers blooms.

Q: Are there any floral trends I should be aware of?

A: These days, big, busy arrangements are largely out; simple, clean bunches of flowers are favored. Think monochromatic (all one color); bright, vivid blooms instead of all pastels; ribbon-tied, compact nosegays instead of huge arrangements trailing ivy. Another cool trend: having the bridesmaids (and even the bride) each carry a few stunning stems (roses, lilies, or other distinctive flowers). A huge bridal bouquet of just baby's breath can also look incredible.

Q: I want to keep my bouquet—do I have to toss it during the reception?

A: You don't have to toss the actual bouquet you carry down the aisle if you don't want to—many brides have their florist create a smaller tossing bouquet, to be given away to a lucky female guest.

staple business card here

CONTACT CHEAT SHEET: Florist

Name: _____

Address: _____

_____

Contact: _____

Phone: _____

Fax: _____

Web site: _____

Estimate $_____

Deposit $_____   Date paid: ____ / ____ / ____

Total cost $_____

Balance $_____   Date due: ____ / ____ / ____

Notes

_____

_____

_____

_____

_____

_____

_____

_____

_____

_____

_____

_____

_____

_____

_____

_____

_____

_____

_____

invitations

The invitations are your guests' first taste of your wedding, so make sure they reflect the spirit, style, and formality of the celebration. Spend some time familiarizing yourself with all the (frighteningly) specific wording conventions and addressing rules—if only to understand what others will expect. (We don't go into minute detail here.) In order to be prepared to send your invitations out at the two-month mark, you'll want to start your search four or five months out. If you are concerned about scheduling conflicts, send a save-the-date card as soon as you nail down your wedding date.

Invitation Style & Elements Worksheet

Style

☐ Formal   ☐ White or ecru paper

☐ Casual   ☐ Handmade or colored paper

Lettering

☐ Traditional type   ☐ Engraving

☐ Modern type   ☐ Thermography

☐ Black ink   ☐ Calligraphy

☐ Colored ink _____   ☐ Letter press

Envelopes/size

☐ Plain envelopes   ☐ Traditional, folded

☐ Decorative envelope linings   ☐ Oversize, unfolded

Wording

☐ Bride's parents as hosts   ☐ Couple as hosts

☐ Groom's parents as hosts   ☐ All parents listed

Names and information to be listed on invitation

Bride: _____

Groom: _____

Bride's parents, stepparents: _____

_____

Groom's parents, stepparents: _____

_____

Wedding date and time: _____

Ceremony site name and address: _____

_____

Reception site name and address: _____

_____

Invitations needed # _____

(Note: number is not equal to guest list; each couple/family will get only one invitation)

Invitation budget $_____

Calling All Stationers

To find a stationer, research large specialty or chain stationery stores, small independent stationers, department store wedding-stationery services (may be associated with bridal registries), and mail-order catalogs. Ordering your invitations online is also a simple (and often cost-effective) option. Log onto **www.TheKnot.com/invitations**.

Make appointments with several stationers:

Name: _____

Address: _____

_____

Phone: _____

Referred by: _____

App't date: ___ /___/___ Time: _____

Price estimate: $_____

Notes: _____

_____

_____

_____

_____

_____

_____

Name: _____

Address: _____

_____

Phone: _____

Referred by: _____

App't date: ___ /___/___ Time: _____

Price estimate: $_____

Notes: _____

_____

_____

_____

_____

_____

_____

Questions to Ask Stationers

☐ Is there a style or type of invitation the store specializes in (traditional styles, theme invitations)?

☐ Are there sample books to browse through? (This will give you a great idea of whether the stationer's work jibes with what you want.)

☐ Does the stationer do custom designs? What about calligraphy? (If there's no in-house calligrapher, they may be able to refer you.)

☐ Does the store have a sample wording guide for you to use to word your invitations? (This is helpful, especially if you're concerned about proper etiquette or have divorced parents, which can make wording complicated.)

☐ Once you place your order, will you be able to see a proof (what the invitation will look like) before the actual invitations are ready?

☐ How long after you place an order will your invitations come in?

☐ What happens if there's an error on the order?

☐ Can you be assured that the stationer will have your invitations printed exactly as you order them (for example, he or she will not change the wording to reflect his or her understanding of rules of etiquette)?

☐ How are invitations priced? Will you get a discount if you purchase other wedding stationery at the same time? Can you get a printed price sheet?

☐ Does the stationer sell other personalized wedding accessories (matchbooks, champagne flutes, napkins, guest books)?

Knot Knowledge: Invitation Tips

What It Costs Prices depend on the kind of invites you choose, where you order them, the ink, the typeface, the printing process, and, of course, how many you need. You'll spend anywhere from $1.50 each to $12 or more each. If you'll hire a calligrapher, factor in that extra cost (call a few for price estimates if you're considering it).

Ways to Save Keep it simple. Top-quality paper and custom-colored inks will jack up the price. So will decorative envelope linings and multiple enclosures. Use response postcards instead of cards and mini addressed envelopes, or set up a toll-free number for guests to call. If you're concerned about postage, stay away from oversize or overweight styles. Opt for thermography over engraving. Work with a large, mainstream stationer or order from a catalog.

Take a Number Don't order the exact number of invites you'll need—get twenty or thirty extra. It's better to have leftovers than to have to reorder later, which can be very pricey. Also order extra envelopes to leave room for addressing errors. (If you're hiring a calligrapher, he or she may ask for a certain percentage of extras.) You'll send one invitation per household (not per guest), but a child over eighteen living at home gets his or her own invite.

Give Me Proof Not to beat you over the head with this, but make sure you check that proof very precisely for spelling, dates, and times. (Double-check the calendar!) Have a smart innocent bystander look it over, too. Any last-minute changes will cost you.

Write On It's customary to handwrite your guests' addresses instead of typing or printing out computer labels. If you've got more guests than your writing hand can handle, get your wedding party to help.

Informal Invites For a small or less formal affair, visit the nearest card store for ready-to-buy invitations and handwrite the information. It's personal, affordable, and perfectly acceptable.

Plan By the Numbers Lightly mark a number on an upper corner of the back of each reply card. Keep a numbered list with corresponding names. When you can't read someone's handwriting, you'll still know whom to expect.

☐ Based on the styles and services available, choose your stationer.

☐ Write out exact invitation wording and get okays from all involved.

☐ Finalize decisions as to:

Type of paper _____

Ink color _____

Type design _____

Style of printing (thermography or engraving) _____

Reception cards _____

RSVP (response) cards _____

Other enclosures (pew cards, in-case-of-rain cards, and so on) _____

Thank-you notes, announcements, ceremony programs, maps, and other stationery _____

_____

☐ Place your order. Review contract or receipt for the following critical points:

- Name and contact information for you and the vendor
- The exact wording of your invitation and all enclosures, printed, with correct line breaks
- The number of:
    invitations _____
    enclosures _____
    envelopes _____
- The return address to be printed on the envelopes, if applicable
- Paper stock and color
- Ink color
- Typeface to be used (a sample should be attached)
- Printing style (thermography, engraving, or other)
- Descriptions and amounts of other wedding stationery ordered
- Descriptions and amounts of any other accessories ordered
- Date the order will be ready
- Total price
- Deposit amount due
- Balance and date due
- Cancellation and refund policy
- Stationer's signature

☐ Proofread the order to make sure all information is factually correct and there are no typos. (Triple-check all locations and addresses.)

☐ Sign contract or receipt.

- ☐ Have the store fax you a proof before the print job is run; proofread carefully and fix any errors.
- ☐ If you want a calligrapher to address your invites, hire one.
- ☐ When your order comes in, count invitations and envelopes and proofread; bring errors to the stationer's attention immediately.
- ☐ If you will include hotel reservation cards and/or maps, get or create them.
- ☐ If you haven't yet, buy thank-you notes and any other stationery.
- ☐ Take a finished invitation to the post office to weigh for proper postage.
- ☐ Mail your invitations two months before the wedding.

ASK CARLEY
Invitation Etiquette & Issues

Q: How do I assemble my invitations?

A: Depending on the style you've chosen, you'll leave them flat or fold them in half or in fourths. The text should be on the front, the fold on the left. Tuck enclosure cards inside, or set them on top of the larger card. Put the pile in an ungummed (inner) envelope, with the print visible upon opening the flap. Leave the inner envelope unsealed. Once you've written the guests' names on the inner envelope, place it inside the outer envelope, with the names facing the flap. Address the outer envelope, seal, and stamp; you're done!

Q: What are the guidelines for inner-envelope addressing?

A: The formal way is with titles only: *Mr. and Mrs. Smith; Ms. Adams and Mr. Zorn* (alphabetically, if a couple has different last names); *Dr. and Mrs. Jones* (if you need to use a professional title). If your wedding is more casual and intimate, you can just use first names or familiar titles *(Aunt Emma)*.

Q: What about the outer envelope?

A: Guests' names and mailing addresses should be written out in full on the outer envelope—*Mr. and Mrs. Paul Daly, Ms. Jacqueline Underberg,* and so on. Spell out *Street, Lane,* and *Apartment.* Your stationer will probably have a booklet all about titles and addressing that will help you with other specific questions you have. You can also find all these details on TheKnot.com.

Q: Do you have to put a return address on the wedding invitations?

A: A return address is a good idea, but you don't necessarily have to have it printed on the envelopes. To save money, handwrite a return address on the back flap. The address should be that of the person whom you've designated to receive response cards—be it the bride's mother, the groom's mother, or the bride and/or groom themselves. The response card envelopes (or the postcards, if you're using them) should be printed with this address.

Q: How are announcements different from invitations, and when are they sent?

A: Announcements are sent to family, friends, and colleagues whom you aren't inviting to the wedding but still want to inform about your marriage. Send them when you've had a very small wedding, or when you want business associates and faraway relatives to be aware that you're now married. Announcements are worded similarly to invitations and are sent on your wedding day. Some recipients may choose to send you a wedding gift; graciously send a thank-you note immediately.

staple business card here

CONTACT CHEAT SHEET: Stationer

Name: _____

Address: _____

_____

Contact: _____

Phone: _____

Fax: _____

Number and type of invitations ordered: _____

_____

Other stationery ordered: _____

_____

Estimate $_____

Deposit $_____   Date paid: ____ / ____ / ____

Total cost $_____

Balance $_____   Date due: ____ / ____ / ____

Calligraphy cost $_____

Notes

_____

_____

_____

_____

_____

_____

_____

_____

_____

_____

_____

_____

_____

CHAPTER SIXTEEN

cake

Your wedding cake should certainly taste great, but it should also turn heads. Have it designed to match your wedding style, echoing your colors, flowers, or theme. You can even have it created to match the bride's dress, with similar detailing or motifs. In general, you can take your time booking the cake, even waiting until the final months before the wedding. Just keep in mind that noted designers—the kind featured in national or big-city magazines—will be booked far in advance.

Wedding Cake Worksheet

Style

☐ Traditional   ☐ Round
☐ Unique   ☐ Square
☐ Ornate   ☐ Cupcakes
☐ Simple

Construction

☐ Sheet cake   ☐ Tiered, with columns
☐ Tiered, stacked   ☐ Tiers # _____

Use   ☐ As a centerpiece   ☐ As primary dessert

Ornamentation

☐ Fresh-flower garnish   ☐ Sugar-flower decorations

☐ Topper_____

Flavors _____

_____

Icing _____

Filling _____

Colors _____

_____

Thematic ideas _____

_____

Groom's cake ☐ Yes   ☐ No

Flavors _____

_____

Thematic ideas _____

_____

Number of slices # _____ (will likely equal # of guests)

Cake budget $_____

Calling All Cake Designers & Bakeries

To find cake designers and bakeries, ask newlywed friends or your caterer, florist, or photographer; use a favorite bakery; or work with the in-house designer at your reception site. Research cake looks you like (try magazines, cake articles on-line or wedding-cake books). Copy, rip out, or print out pictures to bring with you. Log onto **www.TheKnot.com/cake**.

Make appointments with several cake designers/bakeries:

Name: _____

Address: _____

_____

Phone: _____

Referred by: _____

App't date: ___ / ___/ ___ Time: _____

Price estimate: $_____

Notes: _____

_____

_____

_____

_____

Name: _____

Address: _____

_____

Phone: _____

Referred by: _____

App't date: ___ / ___/ ___ Time: _____

Price estimate: $_____

Notes: _____

_____

_____

_____

_____

Questions to Ask Cake Designers & Bakeries

☐ Will the designer create a custom cake, or are there specific styles to choose from? Look at photos and actual cakes, if possible. (Bring pictures if you have a custom cake style in mind.)

☐ What ingredients are used—fresh fruits or purees, Italian butter cream, farm-fresh butter, kosher? (This may or may not be crucial to you, but the better the ingredients, the better a cake will taste! It could also cost more.) Ask for a list of cake flavors and fillings.

☐ How far in advance are cakes prepared? (The closer to your wedding date the better.)

☐ Is there a baker and a designer, or does one person do the entire cake, from batter to sugar flowers? How many people work with the designer? (You'll get an idea of the time it takes the shop to put out a cake. Whether it's a single person or a team of people, however, should have no bearing on quality.)

☐ How many wedding cakes does the shop do a weekend? (This will also tell you how much time the shop puts into each cake.)

☐ If you want to garnish your cake with fresh flowers, will the cake designer work with your florist, or are you responsible for procuring the blooms?

☐ Are cakes priced by the slice or by the cake? Are different flavors or fillings different prices? Will there be extra labor costs if the cake is one of a kind or complex? (Ask for a price list.)

☐ Does the price include the top cake tier, or is it extra? (Our favorite bakers include the top tier—the one many couples save for their first anniversary—for free.)

☐ Is the baker licensed by the state health department? (Very important!)

☐ Does he or she deliver? How much does it cost? (If the cake is large, delicate, or complicated, the extra cost is worth it.)

Knot Knowledge: Cake Tips & Trends

What It Costs Most designers charge by the slice (that is, per guest). Expect to pay between $1.50 and $15 a slice, depending on where you live, the exclusivity of the designer, and the complexity of the cake.

Ways to Save Order a smaller cake that's exactly what you want and several sheet cakes of the same flavor to be cut in the kitchen. Stay away from tiers, handmade sugar flowers, and custom cakes involving special molded shapes. Forgo fondant; butter-cream frosting is less expensive.

Sizing It Up Three standard tiers will probably serve fifty to a hundred guests; you'll likely need five layers for two hundred guests or more (these are guidelines; ask your cake designer for exact numbers). If you'll have a dessert table or other sweets in addition to cake, consider a cake sized for half your number of guests (the servings will be a little smaller).

Flavor Saver Unless you simply can't decide, don't order different flavors by layer. Variety could cost you—and guests don't generally get to choose anyway!

Topper Tips Get creative with your cake topper. Riff on your wedding theme, consider your hobbies, include pictures, make it yourself.

Fresh, Not Fatal If you use fresh flowers, triple-check with your florist that they have not been sprayed with pesticides. Make sure that other decorative elements that are not edible are removed.

Meltaways If you're getting married outdoors in a hot climate, stay away from whipped cream, meringue, and butter-cream icing, which melt!

Homegrown It's a nice personal touch to have your grandmother or mom bake your cake, but this works best for small weddings. Baking for two hundred or more is a feat of engineering best left to the professionals.

Delivery Details Cake delivery will take a little coordination. Complex cakes may not necessarily be delivered ready to go. Make sure there is time and space for assembly to take place. Refrigeration may also be required.

Freezer Burn Eating the top tier of your cake on your first anniversary sounds far better than it tastes, believe us. Instead, indulge on your two-week anniversary—and treat yourself to a fresh cake in the same flavor when you've survived the first year.

Ordering the Cake Checklist

☐ If possible, attend tastings or ask for sample slices to make sure the work of the bakers/designers you're considering looks *and* tastes good.

☐ Book your favorite cake designer by phone. Fax to confirm; include your wedding date.

☐ Finalize decisions as to:

Cake flavor _____

Fillings _____

Icing (butter cream, marzipan, fondant) _____

Decorations (piping, sugar flowers, fresh flowers) _____

Number of tiers _____

Shape _____

Cake topper/finial _____

Number of guests to feed _____

☐ Request a contract or receipt and review for the following critical points:
- Name and contact information for you and the vendor
- Wedding date, time, and location
- When, how, where (complete address of site) and by whom the cake will be delivered (or picked up)
- A detailed description of the cake ordered (including all items listed above)
- A list of anything you're renting (plastic cake tiers, cake stand, and so on)
- Delivery and setup fees
- Total price
- Deposit amount due
- Balance and date due
- Cancellation and refund policy
- Cake designer's signature

☐ Sign contract or receipt.

CONTACT CHEAT SHEET:
Cake Designer & Bakery

Name: _____

Address: _____

_____

Contact: _____

Phone: _____

Fax: _____

Web site: _____

Description of cake: _____

_____

Number of people to feed: # _____

Estimate $_____

Deposit $_____   Date paid: ____ / ____ / ____

Total cost $_____

Balance $_____   Date due: ____ / ____ / ____

Notes

_____

_____

_____

_____

_____

_____

_____

_____

_____

_____

_____

_____

_____

_____

staple business card here

Cake Etiquette & Issues

Q: Why is my reception site charging me a "cake-cutting fee"?

A: If you use a cake designer who is not affiliated with your reception site and/or caterer, you may be charged an additional fee by the establishment to cut and serve the cake. It's an incentive for you to use their in-house baker (and not be charged an extra fee), so if you decide not to, factor in another $1.50 or more per person.

Q: Do we need to serve a dessert besides the cake?

A: We think the wedding cake is dessert enough, but many couples do opt for a table full of éclairs, petits fours, cream puffs, and other delectables. Especially if you choose a very specific cake flavor (cheesecake, dense chocolate, carrot) that not all your guests might like, you may want to offer additional dessert, or perhaps serve ice cream and/or fruit with the cake.

Q: What's a groom's cake?

A: Groom's cakes are a southern tradition. Traditionally they were rich chocolate cakes that complemented the white, light bride's cake (a.k.a. your wedding cake). These days, both cakes can be whatever flavor you like. Go theme-crazy with the groom's, having it made in the shape of a football, a checkerboard, or anything else. The groom's cake is generally taken home by guests in slice boxes. Supposedly, single women who sleep with the slice under their pillows will dream of their future husbands!

Q. When and where do we cut the cake?

A: We adore the idea of having the cake in plain sight on a lighted, decorated table during the entire reception—guests love to look at it! However, it depends on how much space you have (and the weather if the party is outside). Work with your caterer or site manager to determine the timing details. Here's how it unfolds: The bride and groom cut a piece from the bottom tier of the cake together (his hand over hers), slip the slice onto a plate, grab a fork (a waiter or the caterer should be nearby to help), and feed each other a bite. If you want to, you can cut pieces for your parents and use this as an opportunity to thank them. After the required photographs are taken, the banquet manager will take the cake away and have it cut in the kitchen, carrying plates out to each table. Often the bride and groom make a toast or speech at this time.

formalwear

f you're going the traditional route, your basic formalwear decisions will be dictated by the time and formality of the affair. If you're renting, don't wait until the last minute—all the best tuxes will be gone. Plan to reserve all formalwear around the three- or four-month mark and pick it up a few days before the wedding.

Formalwear Worksheet

Source
- ☐ Rental
- ☐ Purchase
- ☐ Closet

General style
- ☐ For evening
- ☐ For daytime
- ☐ Formal
- ☐ Semiformal
- ☐ Informal
- ☐ Current
- ☐ Classic

Tuxedo specifics
- ☐ Tailcoat
- ☐ Cutaway
- ☐ Dinner jacket
- ☐ Mandarin
- ☐ Peaked lapel
- ☐ Notched lapel
- ☐ Shawl lapel
- ☐ ¾-length coat

Suiting colors
- ☐ Black
- ☐ Gray/charcoal
- ☐ Navy
- ☐ White/cream (linen)
- ☐ Other ____

Accessories
- ☐ Vest/waistcoat
- ☐ Cummerbund
- ☐ Bow tie
- ☐ Long tie
- ☐ Cuff links
- ☐ Studs
- ☐ White shirt
- ☐ Ivory shirt
- ☐ Pastel shirt

Color(s) to complement _____

_____

Groom's formalwear budget $_____

Groomsmen's formalwear budget $_____ (each)

Calling All Formalwear Stores

For formalwear rentals, check out chain or independent tuxedo stores or department stores; some bridal salons also rent formalwear. Visit the International Formalwear Association's Web site at www.formalwear.org to find member stores near you.

Make appointments at several stores:

Name: _____   Name: _____

Address: _____   Address: _____

_____   _____

Phone: _____   Phone: _____

Referred by: _____   Referred by: _____

App't date: ___ /___/ ___ Time: _____   App't date: ___ /___/ ___ Time: _____

Price estimate: $_____   Price estimate: $_____

Notes: _____   Notes: _____

_____   _____

_____   _____

_____   _____

_____   _____

Questions to Ask Formalwear (Rental) Stores

☐ Does the store have formalwear in stock for you to try on, or can you only look at styles on mannequins?

☐ What's the starting price? Are there package deals if you rent a certain number of tuxedos?

☐ What's included in a full rental (accessories, pressing, other services)?

☐ Can you buy a tuxedo? What's the starting price?

☐ Are there on-site and/or same-day alterations?

Knot Knowledge: Formalwear Tips

What It Costs The average tuxedo rental is $50 to $200, depending on the style and where you rent from. Rental generally includes a jacket, trousers, shirt, vest or cummerbund, studs, cuff links, and a tie. If you have reason to wear a tuxedo at least two or three times a year, it might pay for you to buy one for your wedding—they run $300 to $700.

Ways to Save Wear a basic black, nondesigner tux. A formal tailcoat or daytime cut-away coat will cost more. If your wedding is semiformal, the groom and groomsmen can wear nice suits they already own. If you're all renting at the same place, you should get a certain amount off, or the groom's rental may be free.

Stand Out in Style The groom should have a slightly different look than the groomsmen. Consider a different-color vest or cummerbund, a different tie or shirt style or color, or a slightly different jacket style (or a white dinner jacket with the groomsmen in black).

Get Comfortable To make sure your formalwear fits correctly, check the following: (1) with arms at sides, the jacket hem is not longer than the tips of your fingers; (2) your shirt just peeks out from the jacket sleeves; (3) the jacket sleeves hit the tops of your hands; (4) your pants touch the heels of your shoes and have a small fold in front over the shoes; (5) you can squat without splitting seams; and (6) you can comfortably lift your arms to just below shoulder height.

Don't Be Colorblind If you and your bride are determined to match the men's accessories (vests, ties) to the bridesmaids' dresses, bring a fabric swatch to the formalwear store or when you go tie shopping.

Wear the Right White If the bride is wearing a pure-white dress, the guys should not wear ivory.

Order All At Once Rent all the groomsmen's tuxedos from the same store. Ask the shop for measurement cards to send to out-of-towners. Make sure they have time to visit the formalwear store a day or so before the wedding for a final fitting.

Pay Their Way Groomsmen pay for their own rentals, but it's a good idea to place one big order and get paid back. Don't rely on everyone to make their own arrangements—it won't happen.

Avoid Tux Shortages If your wedding is around the holidays or during the high seasons for weddings or proms, visit the formalwear store six months in advance.

Return Rules Arrange for someone to return all the tuxes to the shop after the wedding—the best man is a good candidate.

Renting the Formalwear Checklist

☐ Along with the best man, try on styles you like and decide whether the groom's outfit will be slightly different from the rest of the men's.

☐ Make final decision(s) on your formalwear.

☐ Get measured and have the best man and other groomsmen come in to do the same; have out-of-town groomsmen send their measurements.

☐ Decide what size(s) to order. Ask to see the manufacturer's sizing chart yourself. Choose the size that fits each groomsman's largest measurement.

☐ Review your receipt for the following critical points:
- Name and contact information for you and the store
- Your wedding date
- Complete description of what you're renting:

    Names of all groomsmen _____

    _____

    _____

    Designer or manufacturer name(s) _____

    Style numbers _____

    Sizes _____

    Colors _____

    Fabrics _____

    Accessories (vests, cuff links, shoes) _____

    Number of tuxes ordered # _____

- Pickup date
- Return date
- Total price
- Late-return fee
- Deposit amount due
- Balance and date due
- Cancellation and refund policy
- Salesperson's signature

☐ Sign receipt.

☐ If you'll wear any accessories (tie, cuff links, and so on) that don't come with your rental, purchase them.

Groomsmen's Measurements Worksheet

Name: _____

Shoe: _____   Shirt: _____   Coat: _____

Insleeve: _____   Waist: _____   Inseam: _____

Name: _____

Shoe: _____   Shirt: _____   Coat: _____

Insleeve: _____   Waist: _____   Inseam: _____

Name: _____

Shoe: _____   Shirt: _____   Coat: _____

Insleeve: _____   Waist: _____   Inseam: _____

Name: _____

Shoe: _____   Shirt: _____   Coat: _____

Insleeve: _____   Waist: _____   Inseam: _____

Name: _____

Shoe: _____   Shirt: _____   Coat: _____

Insleeve: _____   Waist: _____   Inseam: _____

Name: _____

Shoe: _____   Shirt: _____   Coat: _____

Insleeve: _____   Waist: _____   Inseam: _____

Name: _____

Shoe: _____   Shirt: _____   Coat: _____

Insleeve: _____   Waist: _____   Inseam: _____

Name: _____

Shoe: _____   Shirt: _____   Coat: _____

Insleeve: _____   Waist: _____   Inseam: _____

CONTACT CHEAT SHEET:
Formalwear Store

Name: _____

Address: _____

_____

Contact: _____

Phone: _____

Fax: _____

Store hours: _____

Type and amount of formalwear ordered: _____

_____

Pickup date: ____ / ____ / ____

Return date: ____ / ____ / ____

Total cost $_____

Deposit $_____   Date paid: ____ / ____ / ____

Balance $_____   Date due: ____ / ____ / ____

Notes

_____

_____

_____

_____

_____

_____

_____

_____

_____

_____

_____

_____

_____

staple business card here

Formalwear Etiquette & Issues

Q: Can I wear a tux at my daytime wedding?

A: Ultimately you can wear whatever you want, but bear these guidelines in mind:

- Daytime: If your entire wedding will happen when the sun is up, tuxes are out. For an ultraformal affair, men traditionally sport a morning suit. If the event is formal but not over the top, focus on gray stroller coats or formal suits in shades to suit the season. If it's semiformal, men can simply wear nice suits, and in warm weather, if the setup is casual, you can even wear a sports jacket and trousers.
- Evening: If your reception will begin after 6 P.M. (5:30's fine, too—and in winter you can stretch it even earlier), you can officially don evening wear. If this is a superformal occasion, get ready for white tie, complete with black tailcoats (the top hats and canes can stay in the closet). A formal evening wedding calls for black tie—that means tuxedos or James Bond–style white dinner jackets. If it's a semiformal affair, tuxedos are appropriate, or the guys can just wear nice dark suits.

Q: Is it okay to take my jacket off at the reception?

A: Keep it on during cocktails so everyone can see how dapper you look! It's fine to remove your jacket for the dance floor later (after the first dance, please). If you wear a vest, consider a style with a back instead of one with an adjustable waist and open back—you'll still look put together without your jacket.

Q: Tuxes seem so boring. Are there any ways to dress one up and make it more me?

A: Unique vests and patterned ties make a standard tux special. Pastel-colored shirts are also a trend. Or keep it classic on the cover and go crazy with fun socks, cool boxers and novelty cuff links (all make great groomsmen's gifts). Also consider incorporating elements of your ethnic heritage—with a kilt, a kente cloth accent, or a Chinese silk vest.

Q: I want to wear a tux, but I don't want my guests to have to go out and rent them. How do I let them know they don't have to?

A: Include the phrase "black tie invited" or "black tie optional" on your invitations. This tells male guests that the men in the wedding party are going to be decked out in tuxes, and that they are invited to wear them as well, but that dark suits are just as appropriate. It also clues women in to the fact that they should wear evening gowns or cocktail dresses.

transportation

There are two considerations in the transportation category: luxuries (such as limos for you and your families) and essentials (for example, parking). A limo company can certainly simplify many of your transportation issues in style, but it is a cost you can easily cut. If you have some extra cash for special wheels, go for something classic, fun, or cool—your arrival can set the spirit of the occasion. Try to make transportation arrangements two months before the wedding.

Wedding Wheels Worksheet

Bride & groom arrival and departure style

☐ Stretch limo   ☐ Town car

☐ Classic car   ☐ Luxury car

☐ Horse & buggy   ☐ Own car

☐ Other_____

Attendants and family transportation

☐ Stretch limos (10–12 passenger capacity) #_____

☐ Limos (6 passenger capacity) #_____

☐ Town cars (4–6 passenger capacity) #_____

☐ Own cars

Guest needs

☐ Buses (52 passenger capacity) #_____

☐ Vans (7 passenger capacity) #_____

☐ Parking attendants (you hire)

☐ Valet parking costs (you prepay)

Transportation budget $_____

Transportation Etiquette & Issues

Q: Who's supposed to ride with whom if we hire limousines?

A: It's really up to you. You can go all out and arrange for a limo to get the guys (groomsmen and groom) to the ceremony site, one for the bridesmaids to get from the bride's home (or hotel suite) to the wedding, and one for the bride and her escort. Or, if it's possible for the wedding party to get to and from the wedding locations in their own cars (or by carpooling together or with guests), you might hire just one limousine for the bride and her escort to ride to the ceremony site and then to take the newlyweds to the reception. Sometimes the best man and maid of honor share the ride to the reception with the bride and groom.

Calling All Car Companies

To find limousine or other transportation companies, log onto **www.TheKnot .com/limos.**

Make appointments with several car companies:

Name: _____   Name: _____

Address: _____   Address: _____

_____   _____

Phone:_____   Phone: _____

Referred by: _____   Referred by: _____

App't date: ___ /___/___ Time: _____   App't date: ___ /___/___ Time: _____

Price estimate: $_____   Price estimate: $_____

Notes: _____   Notes: _____

_____   _____

_____   _____

_____   _____

_____   _____

Questions to Ask Car Companies

☐ What car types, sizes, and colors are available? How many people can comfortably fit into one?

☐ What about amenities—TV, telephone, bar, sunroof?

☐ Is there a special wedding package? (If the company specializes in weddings, you may get perks such as balloons or champagne flutes.)

☐ Is the company a member of the National Limousine Association (or another professional association if you're renting a trolley or buses)?

☐ If you contract for multiple cars, can you get a group discount?

☐ Are you responsible for the cost of gas or mileage, or do the cars come with a set amount of free miles and gas?

☐ What does the driver wear? (It may or may not matter to you whether it's formal clothing, but you should still ask so he or she doesn't show up in jeans.)

☐ Can you see a copy of the operating license and insurance certificate?

Knot Knowledge: Transportation Tips

What It Costs You'll probably be charged by the hour (starting at about $60 for a limousine), and there may be a minimum amount of time you need to contract the cars for.

Ways to Save Choose a Lincoln over a limousine. Leave out amenities such as TV and sunroof. Don't "stretch" it—stick with an average-size limo. Give only the bride (or couple) a lift, and have the wedding party carpool.

Bring the Paparazzi Have your photographer ride with you. Those in-car shots are a new classic.

Don't Make 'em Wait You may be able to arrange for just pickup or drop-off service, so drivers won't be sitting around (and getting paid) during the ceremony and reception.

Beware Prom Time If your wedding falls during the holidays or graduation season, you may want to book five or six months before your wedding date.

Give Directions Prepare a call sheet with every name, pickup and drop-off address and time, and detailed directions. Also include an emergency contact number in case the driver gets lost.

Drink Up Stash a split of champagne in the car so you can toast each other on the way to the reception. (If the company has a liquor license, they may provide some.)

To the Wedding If money is no object and you're having an intimate family wedding, send a chauffeured car or other mode of transport for every guest.

Alternative Transport Get a horse and buggy or a sleigh. Ride in a motorcycle and side-car. Brides and grooms we know have taken roller skates, skateboards, scooters, and even a tractor to their weddings.

Hiring the Car Company Checklist

☐ Book a limousine or other transportation company by phone. Fax to confirm; include your wedding date.

☐ Finalize decisions as to:

Number of limos or cars # _____

Style and color of each _____

Additional amenities _____

Wedding package price $ _____

☐ Request a contract and review for the following critical points:
- Name and contact information for you and the vendor
- Date, time, and location of pickup and drop-off points (your home, the ceremony site, the reception site, hotels, other places)
- Type and number of limousines/cars rented
- Amenities supplied with each
- Exact hours cars will be hired for
- If possible, name(s) of driver(s)
- Total cost, including mileage and gas
- Overtime fees
- Deposit amount due
- Balance and date due
- Cancellation and refund policy
- Company representative's signature

☐ Sign contract.

staple business card here

CONTACT CHEAT SHEET:
Transportation

Name: _____

Address: _____

_____

Contact: _____

Phone: _____

Fax: _____

Number and type of cars rented: _____

_____

_____

_____

Estimate $ _____

Deposit $ _____   Date paid: ____ / ____ / ____

Total cost $ _____

Balance $ _____   Date due: ____ / ____ / ____

Notes

_____

_____

_____

_____

_____

_____

_____

_____

_____

_____

_____

_____

_____

big–day details

As you'd expect, the last fourteen days before your wedding can be a total blur! Between your own personal nervousness and all the seemingly countless details to deal with, you might wonder if you're actually going to make it. Here are some cheat sheets to make sure you don't get caught in a last-minute panic.

Delegate The closer your wedding day gets, the more responsibilities and contact with wedding professionals you should assign to attendants and family.

Do It Now Bite the bullet and create the seating chart so that you can hand it off to your reception hall manager or caterer at least two days before the wedding. Decide where to post the directory (or display of table cards) to inform each guest where to be seated.

Take Notes Prepare a day-of package for each vendor. Note any last-minute requests you have made on paper. Also include items they will need on the actual day, in case they forget their copies (for example, the song list for the DJ, special food requests for the caterer, a list of must-get people for the photographer).

Call to Confirm When you call each vendor the day before the wedding, make sure to confirm that they have: directions to and address of site, your day-of contact information (cell phone), and the name of their point person during the wedding. If they sound confused about any of the above information, put it in writing for them and fax it. (We know we've been through all of this before, but we can't stress enough the importance of this last-minute attention to detail.) Also confirm a wedding-day phone number for them (note it on pages 181–82).

Dress Up Several days before your wedding, try on your entire ensemble one last time. Catch any dangling threads or last-minute alterations that are needed on the dress. Confirm the comfort of your underclothes and shoes—don't hesitate to buy replacements if you have any problems.

Be Generous Don't let your gifts for your wedding party, parents, or each other get left off the list because of lack of time. Last-minute gift ideas include: bottles of fine wine, flowers, or gift certificates to favorite restaurants.

Review Rooming It's all too easy for guest accommodations to get confused. Contact each hotel and ask for a listing of all of the rooms booked for your wedding. Make sure all out-of-towners who have made reservations are accounted for. Most important, confirm your own accommodations—so you don't spend your wedding night camped out on a friend's couch!

Meet and Greet Put in a call to each guest who has traveled to attend your wedding, even if you just leave a message at their hotel. Have a list ready of who is arriving, when, and where (including phone number) in case you are absolutely swamped by some prewedding emergency.

Schedule an Early Rehearsal Dinner Talk to the hosts about planning it so that you'll have time to chill out the night before the wedding.

Check the Weather If you're marrying in winter or summer, keep potential blizzards and heat waves in mind and plan accordingly (for example, make sure the church parking lot will be shoveled; double-check the air-conditioning at the reception hall).

Relax If the wedding is in the evening, don't spend the entire day freaking out about it. Deal with last-minute issues that need your attention, but also take some time to relax, get a massage, or even work out.

Make Contact Create a complete wedding contact list to take along on the big day. Lucky you, there's one on pages 181–82.

Don't Overdo Alcohol Even if you're nervous. Especially if you're not eating much (brides and grooms don't get much time alone with their dinner plates), overdoing the alcohol at your own reception could be a truly bad idea. Better: Drink water.

Make the Rounds Even if you have a receiving line, it's a nice gesture to stop at each table to talk to your guests, let them toast you, and pose for their pictures.

Don't Be a Perfectionist Things are bound to go wrong—what you can control is how much you let it bother you. Those tend to be some of the best moments, anyway.

ASK CARLEY

Last-Minute Questions

Q: What time should we start getting ready, and when do we need to be at the ceremony site?

A: Whether you'll get up wedding morning and hop right into your gown or tux depends on what time the festivities begin, of course. The bride should allow about forty-five minutes to get dressed, plus forty additional minutes for hair and makeup (depending on whether your dress goes on over your head or not, you might want to do hair and makeup first). If you must go to a salon or makeup counter, tack on another thirty minutes for travel. The groom needs about half an hour to get dressed and groomed, and he should be at the ceremony site about forty minutes before the wedding starts. The bride should try to arrive about twenty minutes in advance. If pictures will be taken before the ceremony, both of them should be there an hour before.

Q: What if the wrong flowers or cake arrives on wedding day—or worse yet, someone or something doesn't show up?

A: First, try not to wig out. There's not a lot you can do once the day is under way, so in the short run, let the right person know if the order is wrong or do your best to track down a missing vendor. If the professional can provide a quick fix (a rush back to the florist shop or local farmer's market for extra roses, for example), have him or her do so. If not, ask yourself whether you can live with what you've got, and talk to the professional about getting compensated financially for what didn't arrive. Remember that if you have a signed contract that clearly states what you ordered, you're okay; you can either get reimbursed or, if you paid with plastic, have your credit-card company dispute the charge. If someone important—the DJ, the photographer—doesn't show (this scenario is pretty rare, so don't lose sleep over it), ask talented guests to spin some CDs (someone can run for a boom box if necessary) or shoot your ceremony and reception. Do whatever it takes to keep the day running smoothly. You can be angry later; for now, focus on the fact that you're getting married.

Wedding-Day Tipping Worksheet

Wedding workers usually get a gratuity if you're happy with their services. Tips are generally given at the end of the wedding; you might want to designate someone to be in charge of handing them over. Before you start liberally giving out cash, however, check the bill—particularly the catering bill—to see if a gratuity is included. And if you're unsure of the tipping policy at your reception site, talk to the manager for suggestions. Put tips in sealed envelopes to be given to:

	$Amt	#	Total
☐ Ceremony site staff $_____	$_____	_____	$_____
☐ Ceremony musicians $_____ each	$_____	_____	$_____
☐ Banquet manager	$_____	_____	$_____
☐ Maître d' $_____	$_____	_____	$_____
☐ Wait staff $_____ each	$_____	_____	$_____
☐ Bartenders $_____ each	$_____	_____	$_____
☐ Restroom attendant(s) $_____ each	$_____	_____	$_____
☐ Coatroom attendant(s) $_____ each	$_____	_____	$_____
☐ Valet(s) $_____ each	$_____	_____	$_____
☐ Security guard(s) $_____ each	$_____	_____	$_____
☐ Reception musicians	$_____	_____	$_____
☐ Hair stylist	$_____	_____	$_____
☐ Makeup artist	$_____	_____	$_____
☐ Delivery driver(s) $_____ each	$_____	_____	$_____
☐ Limo driver(s) $_____ each	$_____	_____	$_____
☐ _____	$_____	_____	$_____
☐ _____	$_____	_____	$_____

Total cash needed $_____

General Tipping Guidelines

- Club or banquet manager: 15–20 percent of the reception bill (less if there is also a maître d')
- Maître d' or captain: 15–20 percent of the reception bill (less if there is also a banquet manager)
- Wait staff: At least $20 each; maître d' will distribute tips for you
- Bartenders: $25–$40 each
- Restroom and coatroom attendants: 50 cents to $1 per guest
- Valets: 50 cents to $1 per car, or arrange a gratuity with management
- Limo driver(s): 15–20 percent of the total bill (to distribute between them)
- Delivery driver(s) (for flowers, cake, and other items): $10 each
- DJ crew or band members: $20–$25 each
- Hairstylist and makeup artist: 15–20 percent of bill
- Have extra $10 and $20 bills for unexpected occasions

Emergency Kit Checklist

Many a bride (and groom) has been grateful that she—or her maid of honor—had the foresight to bring a last-minute-glitch kit to the ceremony and reception. Just pack this stuff into a bag that can be easily slipped under a pew or head table:

- ☐ Small brush or comb
- ☐ Travel-size hairspray
- ☐ Barrettes, bobby pins, ponytail holder
- ☐ Nail file
- ☐ Safety pins
- ☐ Clear nail polish (for stocking runs)
- ☐ Clear Band Aids
- ☐ Breath mints (Altoids are our favorite)
- ☐ Tums
- ☐ Tissues
- ☐ Small mirror
- ☐ Aspirin or ibuprofen
- ☐ Tampons, pads
- ☐ Krazy Glue (for a broken heel or similar small disasters)
- ☐ White masking tape (a quick fix for hems)
- ☐ Static-cling spray
- ☐ Chalk or Ivory soap (to cover unexpected dress stains)
- ☐ Smelling salts (for fainting episodes)
- ☐ Cellular phone (your own or borrowed)
- ☐ Disposable camera
- ☐ Mini bag of pretzels, PowerBar (for a grumbling stomach)
- ☐ Small bottle of water
- ☐ Dental floss
- ☐ Lavender or chamomile oil (to calm you down!)
- ☐ Asthma inhaler or other medication
- ☐ _____
- ☐ _____
- ☐ _____

Notes

_____

_____

_____

_____

_____

_____

_____

_____

_____

_____

_____

_____

_____

_____

_____

_____

_____

_____

_____

_____

_____

_____

_____

_____

_____

_____

_____

_____

_____

Wedding-Day Phone Contacts

Key player	Home phone #	Cell phone #
Bride's parents:	_____	_____
Groom's parents:	_____	_____
Maid of honor:	_____	_____
Best man:	_____	_____
Bridesmaids:		
_____	_____	_____
_____	_____	_____
_____	_____	_____
_____	_____	_____
_____	_____	_____
_____	_____	_____
Groomsmen:		
_____	_____	_____
_____	_____	_____
_____	_____	_____
_____	_____	_____
_____	_____	_____
_____	_____	_____
_____	_____	_____
Child attendants and their parents:		
_____	_____	_____
_____	_____	_____
_____	_____	_____

Key player	Home phone #	Cell phone #
Ceremony site:	_____	_____
Officiant:	_____	_____
Reception site:	_____	_____
Bridal salon:	_____	_____
Formalwear shop:	_____	_____
Ceremony musicians:	_____	_____
DJ/band:	_____	_____
Caterer:	_____	_____
Florist:	_____	_____
Photographer:	_____	_____
Videographer:	_____	_____
Cake designer:	_____	_____
Limousine:	_____	_____
Hotel(s):	_____	_____

Add Your Own Reminders

appendix

Here's a list of every wedding- and honeymoon-related cost we can think of. Try as best you can to keep track of your expenses as you go along so you are not shocked when the credit card bills arrive post-honeymoon. Use the general estimates from page 14 to start filling in the first column. For an interactive version and line-by-line estimates log onto **www.TheKnot.com/budgeter**.

Wedding Service/Product	Amount Budgeted	Amount Spent
Ceremony	$ _____	$ _____
Site fee	$ _____	$ _____
Officiant fee	$ _____	$ _____
Marriage certificate	$ _____	$ _____
Programs	$ _____	$ _____
Huppah	$ _____	$ _____
Candles	$ _____	$ _____
Aisle runner	$ _____	$ _____
Ring pillow	$ _____	$ _____
_____	$ _____	$ _____
_____	$ _____	$ _____
_____	$ _____	$ _____

Reception $ _____ $ _____

Site fee $ _____ $ _____

Rentals:

    Tent $ _____ $ _____

    Tables and chairs $ _____ $ _____

    Linens and dinnerware $ _____ $ _____

    Dance floor $ _____ $ _____

    Portable toilets $ _____ $ _____

    Delivery and setup fees $ _____ $ _____

    _____ $ _____ $ _____

Food $ _____ $ _____

    Service $ _____ $ _____

    Beverages $ _____ $ _____

    Bartender(s) $ _____ $ _____

Cake $ _____ $ _____

    Cutting fee $ _____ $ _____

    Delivery fee $ _____ $ _____

Wedding clothes $ _____ $ _____

Bridal gown $ _____ $ _____

    Alterations $ _____ $ _____

    Cleaning $ _____ $ _____

Headpiece and veil $ _____ $ _____

Bride's accessories:

    Lingerie $ _____ $ _____

    Shoes $ _____ $ _____

    Gloves $ _____ $ _____

    Purse $ _____ $ _____

    _____ $ _____ $ _____

Hair $ _____ $ _____

Makeup $ _____ $ _____

Manicure(s)	$ _____	$ _____
Pedicure(s)	$ _____	$ _____
Facial	$ _____	$ _____
Massage(s)	$ _____	$ _____
Groom's suit or tux	$ _____	$ _____
Shirt	$ _____	$ _____
Tie	$ _____	$ _____
Vest or cummerbund	$ _____	$ _____
Shoes	$ _____	$ _____
Cuff links and studs	$ _____	$ _____
Groom's grooming	$ _____	$ _____
_____	$ _____	$ _____

Stationery
	$ _____	$ _____
Save the dates	$ _____	$ _____
Invitations and envelopes	$ _____	$ _____
Enclosures:		
Reception invitations	$ _____	$ _____
Response cards	$ _____	$ _____
Maps	$ _____	$ _____
_____	$ _____	$ _____
Calligraphy	$ _____	$ _____
Postage	$ _____	$ _____
Announcements	$ _____	$ _____
Thank-you notes	$ _____	$ _____
Married stationery	$ _____	$ _____
_____	$ _____	$ _____

Flowers and decor
	$ _____	$ _____
Bridal bouquet	$ _____	$ _____
Bridesmaids' bouquets	$ _____	$ _____

Boutonnieres	$ _____	$ _____
Flower girl's flowers	$ _____	$ _____
Corsages	$ _____	$ _____
Ceremony site arrangements	$ _____	$ _____
Centerpieces	$ _____	$ _____
Reception site arrangements	$ _____	$ _____
Delivery fees and setup	$ _____	$ _____
Prop rental(s)	$ _____	$ _____
_____	$ _____	$ _____

Music/Entertainment

Music/Entertainment	$ _____	$ _____
Ceremony musicians	$ _____	$ _____
Cocktail–hour musicians	$ _____	$ _____
Reception band or DJ	$ _____	$ _____
Children's entertainment	$ _____	$ _____
_____	$ _____	$ _____

Photo/Video	$ _____	$ _____
Photography package	$ _____	$ _____
Videography package	$ _____	$ _____
Additional prints or albums	$ _____	$ _____
Additional videos	$ _____	$ _____
Disposable cameras	$ _____	$ _____

Rings/Jewelry	$ _____	$ _____
Bride's ring	$ _____	$ _____
Groom's ring	$ _____	$ _____
Engraving	$ _____	$ _____
_____	$ _____	$ _____

Transportation/Lodging $ _____ $ _____

Limousine or car rental $ _____ $ _____
Guest shuttle or parking $ _____ $ _____
Hotel room(s) $ _____ $ _____
Welcome baskets $ _____ $ _____
_____ $ _____ $ _____

Gifts $ _____ $ _____

Attendants $ _____ $ _____
Parents $ _____ $ _____
Party hosts $ _____ $ _____
Each other $ _____ $ _____
Guest favors $ _____ $ _____
_____ $ _____ $ _____

Honeymoon $ _____ $ _____

Transportation $ _____ $ _____
Accommodations $ _____ $ _____
New clothes or gear $ _____ $ _____
Film, sunscreen, and so on $ _____ $ _____
Spending money $ _____ $ _____

Other $ _____ $ _____

Marriage license $ _____ $ _____
Blood tests $ _____ $ _____
_____ $ _____ $ _____
_____ $ _____ $ _____

Tips, taxes, & overages $ _____ $ _____

                    TOTAL: $ _____ $ _____

Guest List

Here's some space to start making a list of potential guests—all the family members, friends, and colleagues you'd like at your wedding. You can make the official list later—just use this space to jot down names whenever you think of them. Use the first few pages for people you are sure about, the last two for "maybes."

Must-haves

_____	_____
_____	_____
_____	_____
_____	_____
_____	_____
_____	_____
_____	_____
_____	_____
_____	_____
_____	_____
_____	_____
_____	_____
_____	_____
_____	_____
_____	_____

Maybes

_____   _____

_____   _____

_____   _____

_____   _____

_____   _____

_____   _____

_____   _____

_____   _____

_____   _____

_____   _____

_____   _____

_____   _____

_____   _____

_____   _____

_____   _____

_____   _____

_____   _____

Gift Log

Guest's Name	Gift	Thank-You Sent
_____	_____	___/___/___
_____	_____	___/___/___
_____	_____	___/___/___
_____	_____	___/___/___
_____	_____	___/___/___
_____	_____	___/___/___
_____	_____	___/___/___
_____	_____	___/___/___
_____	_____	___/___/___
_____	_____	___/___/___
_____	_____	___/___/___
_____	_____	___/___/___
_____	_____	___/___/___
_____	_____	___/___/___
_____	_____	___/___/___
_____	_____	___/___/___
_____	_____	___/___/___
_____	_____	___/___/___
_____	_____	___/___/___
_____	_____	___/___/___
_____	_____	___/___/___

Guest's Name	Gift	Thank-You Sent
_____	_____	___/___/___
_____	_____	___/___/___
_____	_____	___/___/___
_____	_____	___/___/___
_____	_____	___/___/___
_____	_____	___/___/___
_____	_____	___/___/___
_____	_____	___/___/___
_____	_____	___/___/___
_____	_____	___/___/___
_____	_____	___/___/___
_____	_____	___/___/___
_____	_____	___/___/___
_____	_____	___/___/___
_____	_____	___/___/___
_____	_____	___/___/___
_____	_____	___/___/___
_____	_____	___/___/___
_____	_____	___/___/___
_____	_____	___/___/___
_____	_____	___/___/___
_____	_____	___/___/___

Guest's Name	Gift	Thank-You Sent
		___/___/___
		___/___/___
		___/___/___
		___/___/___
		___/___/___
		___/___/___
		___/___/___
		___/___/___
		___/___/___
		___/___/___
		___/___/___
		___/___/___
		___/___/___
		___/___/___
		___/___/___
		___/___/___
		___/___/___
		___/___/___
		___/___/___
		___/___/___
		___/___/___
		___/___/___
		___/___/___

Guest's Name	Gift	Thank-You Sent
_____	_____	___/___/___
_____	_____	___/___/___
_____	_____	___/___/___
_____	_____	___/___/___
_____	_____	___/___/___
_____	_____	___/___/___
_____	_____	___/___/___
_____	_____	___/___/___
_____	_____	___/___/___
_____	_____	___/___/___
_____	_____	___/___/___
_____	_____	___/___/___
_____	_____	___/___/___
_____	_____	___/___/___
_____	_____	___/___/___
_____	_____	___/___/___
_____	_____	___/___/___
_____	_____	___/___/___
_____	_____	___/___/___
_____	_____	___/___/___
_____	_____	___/___/___
_____	_____	___/___/___

Guest's Name	Gift	Thank-You Sent
		___/___/___
		___/___/___
		___/___/___
		___/___/___
		___/___/___
		___/___/___
		___/___/___
		___/___/___
		___/___/___
		___/___/___
		___/___/___
		___/___/___
		___/___/___
		___/___/___
		___/___/___
		___/___/___
		___/___/___
		___/___/___
		___/___/___
		___/___/___
		___/___/___
		___/___/___

Guest's Name	Gift	Thank-You Sent
_____	_____	___/___/___
_____	_____	___/___/___
_____	_____	___/___/___
_____	_____	___/___/___
_____	_____	___/___/___
_____	_____	___/___/___
_____	_____	___/___/___
_____	_____	___/___/___
_____	_____	___/___/___
_____	_____	___/___/___
_____	_____	___/___/___
_____	_____	___/___/___
_____	_____	___/___/___
_____	_____	___/___/___
_____	_____	___/___/___
_____	_____	___/___/___
_____	_____	___/___/___
_____	_____	___/___/___
_____	_____	___/___/___
_____	_____	___/___/___
_____	_____	___/___/___
_____	_____	___/___/___

photo credits

pages ii, 19, 47, 69, 89, 153: Karen Zieff, Zieff Photography,
www.zieffphoto.com

pages 1, 9, 137: Elizabeth Grubb, E Photography,
www.elizabethphotography.com

page 13: Amy Deputy Photography, www.amydeputyphotography.com

page 16: Sam Velez, Graddy Photography, www.graddyphoto.com

page 34: Kimara, 510-597-1827

pages 35, 57, 111: Elizabeth Messina Photography, www.elizabethmessina.com

page 44: Lyn Hughes Photography, www.lynhughesphoto.com

page 66: Michael Martinez, Martinez Photography, www.martinezphoto.com

pages 81, 161, 175: Missy McLamb Photographers, www.missymclamb.com

page 88: Olivier Lalin Photography, www.weddinglight.com

page 101: Laurie Schneider Photography, www.lschneider.com

page 117: Philippe Cheng, Philippe Cheng Photography,
www.philippecheng.com

page 121: Liz Banfield Photography, www.lizbanfield.com

page 129: Stefanie Riedel Photography, www.stefanieriedel.com

pages 133: Mira Mamon, Mira Mamon Stills Photography, www.miramamon.com

page 145: Paul Kubek, www.paulkubek.com

page 169: Angie Silvy Photography, www.angiesilvyphotography.com

Additional chapter opening photos provided courtesy of:
pages 1, 16: Susan Beard Design Studio, Philadelphia, PA; (215) 482-9594

page 3: David Max Steinberg-Amy Vanneman/The Light House, Martha's Vineyard, MA; (508) 693-4460

pages 14, 15, 19: Cappy Hotchkiss, New York, NY; (212) 496-6024; cappyh@earthlink.net